Nearing Death Awareness

of related interest

Attending to the Fact – Staying with Dying
Hilary Elfick and David Head
Foreword by Andrew Hoy
Edited by Cynthia Fuller
ISBN 978 1 84310 247 2

Dealing with Death
A Handbook of Practices, Procedures and Law
Second edition
Jennifer Green and Michael Green
ISBN 978 1 84310 381 3

**Making Sense of Spirituality in Nursing and Health
Care Practice**
An Interactive Approach
Second edition
Wilfred McSherry
Foreword by Keith Cash
ISBN 978 1 84310 365 3

The Inspiration of Hope in Bereavement Counselling
John R. Cutcliffe
Foreword by Ronna Jevne
ISBN 978 1 84310 082 9

On Death, Dying and Not Dying
Peter Houghton
ISBN 978 1 84310 020 1

The Social Symbolism of Grief and Mourning
Roger Grainger
ISBN 978 1 85302 480 1

Nearing Death Awareness

A Guide to the Language, Visions, and Dreams of the Dying

Mary Anne Sanders

Jessica Kingsley Publishers
London and Philadelphia

First published in 2007
by Jessica Kingsley Publishers
116 Pentonville Road
London N1 9JB, UK
and
400 Market Street, Suite 400
Philadelphia, PA 19106, USA

www.jkp.com

Library of Congress Cataloging in Publication Data
Sanders, Mary Anne.
    Nearing death awareness : a guide to the language, visions and dreams of the dying
/ Mary Anne Sanders.
        p. cm.
    Includes bibliographical references.
    ISBN 978-1-84310-857-3 (pb)
    1. Death--Psychological aspects. 2. Terminally ill--Psychology. 3. Terminal
care--Psychological aspects. 4. Death--Religious aspects. 5. Terminally ill--Religious life.
6. Terminal care--Religious aspects aspects. I. Title.
    BF789.D4S25 2007
    155.9'37--dc22

                                        2006100080

British Library Cataloguing in Publication Data
A CIP catalogue record for this book is available from the British Library

ISBN 978 1 84310 857 3

Printed and bound in the United States by Thomson-Shore, Inc.

To my mother

Contents

Acknowledgments

My greatest thanks goes to my mother, Ruth Murphy, who was the single most powerful inspiration in the creation of this book. Though she was unaware of the helpfulness of her NDA behavior on a conscious level at the time, I firmly believe that on a subconscious level she knew of her role in providing invaluable first-hand knowledge to her daughter, enabling a predetermined goal to be obtained within my life plan. For that selfless and potent teaching, I will be eternally grateful.

To my dear husband, Clay, a heartfelt thanks for all of your unfailing support and efforts in this endeavor. Without your consistent encouragement, patient proofreading, and team-player attitude, this book would not have been possible.

A special thanks goes to the faculty and staff of Atlantic University in Virginia Beach, Virginia, for their assistance in my Masters thesis on the topic of NDA on which this book was based. Individual appreciation is extended to my advisors Mark A. Thurston, PhD, and Henry Reed, PhD, for their enthusiasm, encouragement, and efforts to challenge me in the areas of the transpersonal and spirituality. Also to my dear friend Diane Shenk, J.D., R.N., for her support and unfailing belief in the project.

Introduction

RUTH: "My mother is here. Are my suitcases packed?"

MARY ANNE: "Where are you going, mama?"

RUTH: "I'm going home. But I need to know if I'm supposed to change planes."

In the fall of 2004, I had this exchange with my 80-year-old mother while she was under hospice care and actively dying. At first, I thought these were remarks that were either drug-induced or from oxygen deprivation. I also considered the possibility that her decade-old dementia was worsening. But the purpose in my mother's voice and urgency in her eyes told me that there was something more happening. Up to that point the hospice staff had been helpful in educating me in what to expect from the dying process in terms of physical signs, such as delayed breathing, excessive sleep, and skin lividity. But none of their literature prepared me for the shock of witnessing extraordinary near-death behavior or for the opportunity to explore the spiritual value that can be drawn from these extraordinary occurrences. Thus began my study of Nearing Death Awareness (NDA), a behavioral phenomenon that I believe has strong implications for continued existence beyond physical life as we know it. As I began exploring what was in print, I quickly became aware of a blind spot in how professional caregivers prepare both the dying and their families for these unusual but common occurrences, which are exceptional opportunities for spiritual support and growth.

The act of dying appears to be viewed by most of humanity as primarily a sad physical event that may, or may not, depending on their belief system, have spiritual significance. I have learned, however, that it is actually an experience that involves all of the essence of being human: physical, mental, and spiritual. Once they sense the imminence of death, some people begin to view this time as a wondrous gift, when they can examine who they really are, explore their spirituality and grow in love and self-acceptance. As the dying begin an overview of their lives and how they have interacted with others, the learning process continues, resulting in a broader understanding of a more transcendent world. As author David Kuhl stated, "It can be said that they have not only lived fully but also died well" (Kuhl 2002, p.291). A paradox seems to exist for humanity in that a person can seem to grow dramatically in a spiritual sense as the physical self gradually but decisively shrinks (Byock 1997, p.233). Thankfully, this spiritual process is overpowering, and from my perspective, presents the potential for spiritual joy as the dying one lets go, transcending what we perceive as reality, and journeying into yet another dimension of life.

From my research on NDA, I have come to the conclusion that as death nears, quiet but dramatic transformations can surface both mentally and spiritually. Author Kathleen Dowling Singh refers to profound psychospiritual transformations as "grace in dying." Observations, words, and experiences offer a growth in awareness, a universal property of death itself (Singh 2000, pp.2, 5). The unique behaviors of the dying, however, such as peculiar language, purposeful staring, and descriptions of odd dreams, can be quite unsettling and worrisome to witnesses. Often, family, friends, and caretakers respond with annoyance and frustration. They hesitate to discuss it, for fear of appearing "strange." Others simply ignore the behavior, missing a potentially treasured time of connection with the dying and opportunity for spiritual maintenance and personal reflection. Sadly, these inappropriate responses to the dying only promote in them feelings of being alone and misunderstood, with a fear that they may be told, "Don't talk about that!" Spiritual discomfort and confusion may result for all involved. The solution is for those near the dying to be listeners and supporters. This can be more daunting than it sounds; the dying seem to speak in riddles, and act in nonsensical ways at times. The challenge to those in attendance is not only to respect the behavior, but also to put effort into unearthing the important veiled meaning that may lie underneath.

The messages offered by the dying through symbol or suggestion can sometimes convey concepts that serve to secure a peaceful death, provide comfort for loved ones, and even present fleeting moments of awareness of other universal dimensions. Maggie Callanan and Patricia Kelley, in their groundbreaking work, *Final Gifts* (1997), state that the messages fall into two categories: attempts to describe the dying experience as it occurs, and requests for someone or something necessary for a serene death. The first category depicts patient experiences, such as being with one who is deceased, needing to prepare for travel to another place unseen to others, and apparent foreknowledge of the time of their own death. The second category includes the need for forgiveness, reconciliation, and particular people or things required for peaceful closure. In these two types of messages, the dying might refer with a sense of wonder to a beautiful world dawning where deceased loved ones or religious figures are waiting. The dying may share that they can talk to or sense people that are unseen to us (Callanan and Kelley 1997, pp.14–19).

The famous psychoanalyst Carl Jung claimed that when we age, "the more veiled becomes the outside world, steadily losing in colour, tone, and passions, the more urgently the inner world calls us" (Jacobi 1962, p.149). This can also describe the time of "actively dying." In my view, when NDA occurs, both the dying and those present are looking through the peephole of God's door during a sacred moment of wonder. It is during this holy juncture that all may be aware that death is not final and can be a peaceful instead of frightening process. Jung stated that the dying move inevitably toward a "state of diminished consciousness," where they are capable of traveling between normal orientation in this reality and to a new, unknown realm (Jacobi 1962, p.85). The dying can possess the seemingly extraordinary ability to shift from moments of odd reverie and bewilderment to times of extreme clarity. This behavior could quite possibly be living proof that a gradual change is taking place – that of "practice runs" in crossing back to the home of their Creator, then returning to earthly reality for the time being.

While witnessing my mother's NDA behaviors in hospice care, I was simultaneously working on a Masters degree in transpersonal studies, concentrating on spiritual guidance mentorship. The universe seemed to be strategically putting pieces together, firmly leading me to discover first-hand that there is a distinct connection between NDA and spirituality, and that when one either experiences or witnesses NDA, the potential is enormous for everyone involved to delve into what they personally believe. Personally, I already had a belief in an afterlife and the ability of a Higher Power to communicate through different levels of consciousness, specific situations, and other people. But to have had the opportunity to witness confirmation of those beliefs through one that I loved was quite powerful, and was one of the most overwhelmingly influential experiences I have ever had. As a result, I was able to clarify my personal beliefs, but more importantly, I now believe that I possess a stronger faith and no longer perceive death as the terrible demon that we all must face to get to the next stage of existence.

I have written this guide to address the topic of NDA as a potential vehicle of spiritual growth for those that face impending death, as well as for their families, friends, and caregivers. This book is related to, but is not limited by, the particular belief system of its reader. It is also offered to those who are not currently dealing with death, but who will surely do so at some point their future, whether personally or with others. I hope that by gaining increased awareness of the inherent purpose of these behaviors, all that are alert to the Near-Death Experience (NDE) will obtain a more enhanced sense of personal spirituality, and possibly a more expansive view of existence beyond reality. One may then be able to view the NDA experience from a larger context: as an example of how we are all connected within the universe. I see us as an integral part of the Divine, and this experience as a way to grow in intimacy with our Creator. Also, one can recognize consciousness as a multi-layered continuum through which the dying pass, progressing from one conscious realm to another. For those who have no particular spiritual beliefs, knowledge of these patterns of behavior will, at the least, enable response with open-minded support to the dying as they exhibit it. Perhaps most importantly, I would like to think that all readers will experience a greater sense of peace, acceptance, and hope, knowing that death is not the end, but a time of graduation to continued fulfilling existence within the universe.

What is Nearing Death Awareness?

Nearing Death Awareness (NDA), a term coined by two hospice nurses, Maggie Callanan and Patricia Kelley, refers to the special communications made by the dying near the end of their lives. As death draws closer, the dying seem to develop a unique sensitivity and awareness of persons, places, and things around them. This awakening gradually progresses and increases as they appear to shift from a consciousness of this physical plane to a numinous plane of existence previously unknown. Since the key words were "awareness," "nearing," and "death," the choice of name was developed and introduced in *Final Gifts: Understanding the Special Awareness, Needs and Communications of the Dying* (Callanan and Kelley 1997, pp.28–30).

During these unique occurrences, the dying may appear distracted, preoccupied, and even somewhat bewildered.

They may stare at one place, converse with an invisible person, reach out into the air, or seem generally intent on something unseen. Puzzling dreams and unusual language may occur. During these moments, they usually possess a calm demeanor, or even a matter-of-fact attitude that what is happening is perfectly normal to them. But to family, friends, and caregivers who are unfamiliar with end-of-life care and unprepared to respond helpfully, the dying may appear to be mentally confused due to a variety of possible reasons, such as dementia, low oxygen intake, or medication side-effects.

The NDA experience cannot be proven empirically, but that proof is unnecessary to the one who has "proven" it by personal experience. Such personal experiences have been widely recorded. Some skeptics may scoff at the lack of scientific proof of NDA accounts. However, knowledge can yet be attained beyond what is sensed with our eyes and ears. There is a mysterious central energy that many of us tap into in a spiritual sense. Author Rachel Naomi Remen, MD has said "Much of life can never be explained but only witnessed" (Remen 1997, pp.300–1). She continues by proposing that "Life is best defined by mystery." Even though our culture is into control and mastery of all situations, mystery presents us with the living experience of the sacred. This cannot be measured, putting it beyond the reach of science. But life is larger than science, and when in the presence of mystery, life becomes larger (Remen and Toms 2001). The NDA experience is intensely full of mystery: strange language, visions of beings, odd dreams, etc. If one understands what is possibly occurring during these dramatic processes, these can be serene, comforting, and fulfilling moments, but those who reject the mystery in NDA lose the exceptional opportunity to experience a potentially sacred moment that can strengthen and awaken themselves as well as the one dying.

NDA occurs when people are slowly expiring due to progressive illnesses such as cancer, lung disease, or AIDS. While the dying remain inside their fading physical body, they seem gradually to become aware of a realm that lies beyond and drift between the two dimensions. P.M.H. Atwater, Near-Death Experience (NDE) researcher and author, states:

> Usually, about twenty four to thirty six hours before the death event, the individuals relax and are at peace. They often appear "high" on something because of their unusual alertness, confidence, and sense of joy. They exude a peculiar strength and positive demeanor as if they were now ready for something important to happen. (Atwater 1988, p.189)

The NDA process does not always produce visible physical change, and people do not always appear to be nearing death. They still have blood pressures, breath, pulses, and continue to be able to articulate thoughts. They may speak of being in two places at the same time or somewhere midway between the two (Callanan and Kelley 1997, pp.14–19). Talk of an upcoming trip or change in surroundings can often be relayed to those nearby. In NDA, while completely awake, the dying are often aware of and converse with loved ones who have passed on, or cherished spiritual figures. These familiar faces are usually perceived by the dying as being with them to reassure and assist in what lies ahead.

When hallucination is taking place, one is completely out of touch with surroundings. The dying person undergoing

NDA, however, stays alert to both ordinary reality as well as the alternate reality and can switch effortlessly between the two (IANDS 2006a). The person can cease conversation with a deceased relative or spiritual being and quickly pay attention to what is taking place in the room. The dying person never appears to see living, absent relatives in their visions. But people who the patient believes to be alive sometimes do appear if they have actually died since the time the patient last had contact with them. Spiritual healer and psychic, Mary T. Browne, tells of her experiences with the dying:

> I always know their time is close when they start telling me they're seeing people who have previously gone over, sometimes having long conversations with [them]… These are not hallucinations. The spirit body is simply beginning to make the transition. The patient can genuinely see the spirits who are waiting for him. Being half on the earth and half in the world of spirit, the dying person begins to relate to both worlds. Just as it takes time to give birth to a soul, it takes time to leave the earth. Death is birth into the realm of the spirit. (Browne 1994, p.9)

The dying can relay to others what they are experiencing even if unable to speak, in ways of messaging beyond that of words. Frequently, they will be observed smiling, waving, nodding, even laughing, or reaching for something or someone unseen. They may aimlessly pick at their bedding and restlessly attempt to get out of bed. These non-verbal communications can be interpreted as illustrations to the dying as well as witnesses that the dying do not perceive themselves to be alone. Rather, they perceive that others from beyond have arrived to meet them for their journey. Those gathered by the deathbed can find comfort in these unseen reunions, and can perceive suggestions of life beyond what they presently know. Psychic Edgar Cayce referred to these reunions: "Thus, the communion of saints means that all who have one purpose, whose thoughts and motivative forces are one, may communicate; whether those in the material plane, in the borderland, or those that may be upon the shores of the other side of life" (Frejer 1999, p.15). Perhaps the NDA process illustrates that "borderland" that Cayce refers to.

As death draws near, the dying often systematically begin work on several tasks. First, they may begin a life review, perusing the events that they underwent in their lives and often paying particular attention to those that involved relationships with others. From this, a need for taking care of unfinished business may surface, so forgiveness and/or reconciliation may become a strong desire for them. Sometimes for the first time, the dying may begin to look for prevailing themes in their lives, a dramatic first step in spiritual evaluation. A powerful need to harvest lessons learned and contributions made can emerge, revealing how well some beliefs were put into action and effectively lived. Finally, saying farewell to all facets of this world becomes their final goal, one that they naturally accept. This is often demonstrated by their drifting away from previous activities and responsibilities, such as parenting, financial duties, personal hygiene, watching favorite TV programs, etc. The process of NDA can be invaluable when closure is needed to resolve personal issues with others. The visions and dreams that commonly occur in NDA seem to allow the patient to achieve a sense of reconciliation with other individuals, and begin to accept a peaceful departure from life as they know it into a new level of existence.

Interestingly, depending on their physical circumstances, some dying people appear to have "inside information" as to when their demise will actually take place. Some may even be capable of naming the actual day and time of their leaving. Again, the theme of optimal closure emerges, and many illustrate their conviction that death will be a more serene event under specific conditions, and until those conditions are met, they may postpone their deaths. Some may wait for certain individuals to leave the room, while others may wait for the arrival of special family members or friends. The dying may also postpone death until they feel that their loved ones are receiving adequate support from others around them. Once people, circumstances, and issues are in their proper place, death is broached with quiet acceptance. In contrast, the dying may seem at times capable of hastening their deaths. They may perceive their passing at a particular time as a practical way of sparing their families unnecessary pain and inconvenient time out from their own personal lives.

What author Kathleen Dowling Singh refers to as "Nearing Death Experience" adequately describes NDA, in that it is an extraordinary moment in the journey of humanity, a universal transition. As the body dissipates, Singh believes that the dying become aware of a separate sense of self and yet a greater sense of spiritual connection. States of consciousness expand as qualities such as withdrawal, silence, transcendence, and merging gradually occur. The surfacing of these states suggests their source is a higher power, and that a remarkable shift into an expanded state of consciousness and being takes place (Singh 2000, pp.7–12). Edgar Cayce put it thus:

> Thus it [humankind] is made to be ever as one with
> the Father, never losing its identity. For, to lose its
> identity is death indeed – death indeed – separation
> from the Creative Force. The soul may never be lost,
> for it returns to the One Force, but knows not itself
> to be itself any more. (Frejer 1999, p.117)

The moments of NDA are sacred ones for both the dying
and their witnesses. It is my belief that all are exposed to a
holy glimpse into the transcendent world of continued existence. Here we are given an awe-inspiring foretaste of the
powerful, luminous state of Oneness we all share. Whether
specifically expressed through the unique language, visions,
or dreams of the dying, a tremendous opportunity presents
itself for the patients and their witnesses to re-examine their
physical existence, make peace within the soul, and view the
expansive reality beyond.

2

Symbolic Language

> If people would listen more to their own intuitive
> spiritual quadrant...they would begin to compre-
> hend the beautiful symbolic language that dying
> patients use when they try to convey to us their
> needs, their knowledge and their awareness.
> (Kübler-Ross 1991, p.60)

When a dying person speaks in symbolic language, the
moment can be a challenging one for loved ones and
healthcare workers. The words can evoke feelings of fear,
impatience and/or bewilderment for those standing at the
bedside. What is important to remember, however, is that
within those seemingly enigmatic words is a specific intent,
a message to others from the patient experiencing Nearing
Death Awareness (NDA). In order to respect the individual
adequately when this extraordinary behavior occurs, we
must *listen* rather than simply *hear*. The words are pregnant
with meaning and have potential for enhanced communion
with the dying one. Consider these documented examples:

"Mary's going to miss the boat!"

"Sam doesn't know about the trip."

"Are my shoes at the door?"

(Kraybill 2005)

"It's time to get in line."

"Where's the map?"

(Callanan and Kelley 1997, pp.5, 69)

"Go get my airline tickets."

"I hear the train coming!"

"It's a big black beautiful car."

"Hitch them up, it's time to go."

"They've given me a ticket for the bus."

"The boat is here for me."

"Pack my suitcase."

"I'm getting a different place."

(Wooten-Green and Champlin 2001, pp.69–83)

Newspaper staff writer Valerie Reitman once wrote an article about her brother:

> My brother took more trains, planes, and automobiles in the last week of his life than he had taken in months, perhaps years. Those journeys were all the more surprising because they occurred in an intensive-care unit at the end of his three-year battle with bone marrow cancer... Though very weak, Kenny, 45, intermittently recognized and chatted

lucidly with family gathered by his bedside. But he would drop in news of his varied travels: he had gone skiing one afternoon in Australia, he told us, stopped by North Carolina another day, and more than once, had been "stuck in passport control." (Reitman 2004, p.1)

Kathy Pollard, Educational Director for Hospice of the Valley in Phoenix, Arizona, once had an elderly woman touch her cheek and ask, "Oh, my dear – isn't the train we're on beautiful?" Pollard replied by asking if the lady was on the train. The woman replied yes, they both were, and that she was headed to South Dakota. Pollard inquired what would happen when she got there. The woman answered, "Well, my dear, then the journey will be over" (Reitman 2004, pp.1–2).

If these words from bedridden patients with a terminal illness are taken literally, they seem like the hallucinatory ramblings of deteriorating minds. Often, NDA symptoms are attributed to other clinical situations such as delirium, side-effects of medication, or psychiatric illness. And indeed, there *are* situations with patients where forms of dementia and psychosis may be witnessed and identified. But those vocally exhibiting NDA behavior will usually present themselves with themes of strong intent, specifically in the form of metaphorical language. Unfortunately, many times the response is to ignore, argue with him/her, make a joke of the comments, or provide medication to relax the patient. As a result, the dying can feel ashamed, fearful, frustrated, or just simply alone. But if one examines the language in a symbolic sense rather than straightforwardly, those nearby can become more aware of the specific desires and needs of the patient, as well as gain greater knowledge of what the death experience actually feels like (Kraybill

2005). A significant opportunity presents itself; the dying can become the teacher for the living. Just as Jesus used metaphor-packed parables in his teachings, and present-day ministers and spiritual teachers dispense stories to illustrate their points, symbolic communication can be a dramatically effective tool to share unseen knowledge.

The language of symbols is usually what is taking place when the dying appear to speak oddly during NDA. Past personal experiences, typical expressions, and familiar objects or gestures often become illustrative metaphors to express what they are thinking and are concerned about. These attempts to communicate with us are best understood in the context of the patient's life and what he or she has experienced. But more often than not, the dying will utilize the metaphor of travel as a signal to those around them that groundwork for death is being formed within. In fact, the theme of going somewhere is a logical method of expressing their imminent change in spatial location – to die and move on to another phase of existence. This common theme may be presented by the use of planes, cars, boats, horses, or trains. Suitcases gotten out of the attic, bills paid and mailed, housework done, or an upcoming move to another house or city may be cited symbolically as upcoming and necessary preparations.

I recently presented a seminar to staff members at a Cincinnati, Ohio nursing home on the topic of NDA. A staff nurse shared some symbolic language that she witnessed: "My grandfather was passing. He told us to get his suitcase. His mother and father were waiting for him at the school bus to go home." The facility's nursing supervisor told me this: "There was a woman here with both side rails fully up on her bed. She skinned her shins from knees to ankles trying (she said) to get to the end of the lane. Before noon that day, she made it to the end of the lane."

On many occasions, the final words of those about to die can be loaded with colorfully relevant metaphor that correspond to personal life experiences. For his final communication, L. Frank Baum, author of *The Wizard of Oz*, said, "Now I can cross the Shifting Sands." Baum was obviously making reference to the impassable desert surrounding the Land of Oz in his series of books. In 1870 the last words of General Robert E. Lee, Commander of the Army of Northern Virginia in the American Civil War, were, "Strike the tent." Shot in error by his own troops at the Battle of Chancellorsville, Confederate General Thomas "Stonewall" Jackson was said to have murmured right before his death, "Let us cross over the river and sit in the shade of the trees." Russian-born Anna Pavlova, one of the most famous of all ballerinas, stated before her dying in 1931, "Get my swan costume ready." The American theatrical producer Florenz Ziegfeld Jr., dramatically offered these parting images right before his death in 1932: "Curtain! Fast music! Light! Ready for the last finale! Great! The show looks good, the show looks good!"

Sometimes, however, the messages relayed through symbolic language are conveying that the dying one is having difficulty moving on to a peaceful death, and that something needs to be done before serenity can be achieved. This is a time for the family to go back and look again at what is important to the patient and what could possibly be amiss. Callanan and Kelley, in their book, *Final Gifts*, tell the story of Bertha, a dying patient who was agitated one day:

"I can't find the feed for the horses!" she said. "Why do the horses need feed?" she was asked. "I'd *never* make them take me on this trip without feeding them first!" (Callanan and Kelley 1997, p.162)

Bertha was raised on a farm in the North Carolina hills, when transportation was a horse and wagon. Her expression of frustration about the horse feed signaled an unresolved issue.

An African-American Baptist woman was suffering from advanced lung cancer when she was admitted to the palliative care unit. Mild sedation was not helpful in calming her extreme agitation. One day she said, "I'm dirty" repeatedly, along with other phrases suggesting that she needed bathing, so the nurses gave her several bed baths. As the woman's cries continued, her nurse learned from consulting the woman's chart that she had a history of sexual abuse in addition to unresolved fears about salvation. The chaplain was contacted, and performed a "cleansing ritual" based on the woman's belief in baptism for the remission of sins. The woman then became calm, and peacefully died two days later (Endlink 2006). Thanks to the extra effort made by her nurse to decipher the meaning of her symbolic language and address her inner pain, the woman received appropriate spiritual care, which enabled healing and a serene death.

The personal vocation and lifestyle of the dying can be reflected and used in their symbolic expressions to others of unfinished business. For instance, Claude, a former accountant suffering from melanoma, stated to his family, "I can't find the program, so the system won't work!" George, a military serviceman who frequently traveled, spoke of his need for his papers and passport. Dick, an engineer, was undertaking a complex problem when he said, "I'm trying to figure out how to take the house with me and everything in it!" (Callanan and Kelley 1997, pp.81–3, 161–2, 168).

My mother, a retired college secretary and responsible person both with family and finances, made several symbolic statements to me while in hospice care that were packed with metaphor:

> "I need my checkbook. I have to make sure all of my bills are paid."

> "There's a document no one can find in my office at the college. I'm the only one who knows about it and what to do. I've got to take care of it."

These statements would appear normal on the surface except for the fact that I had been controlling her finances for quite some time, and that she had been retired from her college position for 14 years. On another occasion, she angrily informed me that she was being moved to another bed upstairs (the hospice was a one-floor building). When I asked her why she was being moved, she replied, "I don't know, but I don't like it one bit!" Interestingly, this was during the period when she seemed to be in a denial stage of her physical condition. I interpreted her remarks to be communicating her unwillingness to accept her probable death and subsequent potential trip up to "heaven," a place that she firmly believed in.

In preparation for this guide, I obtained copies of daily records kept by hospice workers during my mother's time of "active dying" when she was under 24-hour watch. She made several symbolic comments to nurses and nurse-aides that were noted in her record, often occurring at night. Unfortunately, the remarks were usually referred to as "confused," "agitated," or "hallucinatory," and occasionally the medical response was to administer medication to relax her. Here are some exchanges recorded:

> NURSE: Patient asked if I could take her home. I replied that I'm not allowed to do that. Patient asked me if I could call the phone company for her. When asked why, she said, "I forgot my mother's number, and I want to call her." (Her mother died 39 years ago.)

> NURSE: Patient tried to get out of bed. She stated, "I need to go shut off the car and the gas."

> NURSE: Patient has been insisting that "there is a dead baby in the room. It needs to be removed. I can't get anyone to listen to me!"

The exchange between the two regarding going home and her deceased mother was significant. A few nights before, my mother had tried to get out of bed, saying that her mother was out in the hall and had come to take her home. This consistency with language and a vision implied to me that it is possible that she had been receiving communication and encouragement from her mother from a dimension beyond what we can see. The second comment about shutting off the car and the gas correlated with the emotional situation that appeared to be churning within her that particular day. She had shared with the chaplain that she was not ready to die, and did not want to leave her family. Perhaps shutting off the car and gas was a way of expressing her intent to refrain from dying and moving forward into another dimension of life. Indeed, a few days later, when her sister and I told her that it was OK for her to go, she answered, "I don't think I'm as sick as you think I am."

The last remark about the "dead baby," though graphic and seemingly ridiculous, still held meaning. A few days earlier, the nurses had told me that my mother had asked them what it was like to have a baby, and that she had never experienced it before. My later interpretation was that she was using her previous life experience of childbirth to represent the process of dying, something she'd never experienced. In later describing the baby as dead, this too seems to reflect her attitude that death for her was a dead issue, and that she was determined not to go anywhere, but remain on this earthly plane. Indeed, she actually got her wish and did temporarily overcome death. As of writing, though still unable to care for herself, my mother's health has improved dramatically, NDA behaviors have disappeared, and she has returned to her former normal mental state, giving me permission to share her story.

Symbolic language is sometimes offered by the dying to express their need to "make things right" with either a particular person, specific situation, or a Higher Power. When the desire for forgiveness and/or reconciliation has been relayed by the patient metaphorically, those nearby can best serve the dying by attempting to do what is necessary for the wishes to be achieved, therefore supporting a more peaceful death. Author and hospice chaplain Ron Wooten-Green told of a dying man named Carl who was estranged from his son, Freddie. When asked what he would like to pray for, Carl replied, "That Freddie and I can go around on the carousel." Although a carousel is not a mode of travel, Carl appeared to be expressing that Freddie and he needed to go around and around together, and that he wanted to attempt to relate one more time with his son. A reunion did take place, and Carl passed away peacefully 48 hours later (Wooten-Green and Champlin 2001, pp.95–7).

Wooten-Green also shared the story of Harley, a dying carpenter, whose mentally challenged son named Mick had worked with him and been largely dependent on his father. After Mick threatened suicide, Harley asked Mick to bring him a hammer and nails. When Mick asked his father what he was supposed to do with them, Harley replied repeatedly, "Mick, keep on hammering on the wall," over and over until he took his final breath. This seemed to be Harley's way of saving his son's life by telling Mick not to give up (Wooten-Green and Champlin 2001, pp.15–23).

Hospice nurse Corrine Anderson told the story of her father, A.J., who was dying at the age of 83 of prostate cancer. One evening before his death, A.J. told his daughter that he was going on a big trip and needed to get the "old car" ready. The "old car" was a 1932 Ford sedan that he had always done maintenance on most of the time that Corrine could recall. She quickly identified that this was a portion of life closure for him, with his trip being a metaphorical expression of his upcoming encounter with death. A.J. mimed in bed with his arms and hands moving, his precise preparations apparent on the old car. He would talk with "Bill," a mechanic who had died years before. At one point, A.J. became agitated and said that he had five screws that he couldn't put in. Corrine called her brother, who often worked with their father on the old car, and when he arrived, the brother took the screws, working with his father until A.J. surveyed "the car" and said that it was "ready to go." Since A.J. had five children, the family later mused that handing the five screws to the brother was a symbolic completion of his responsibilities as a father (Anderson 2002, pp.180–183).

Dying people seem to know that they are dying, whether they have been informed or not. But there are some who are able to tell others exactly when they will die, as will be discussed in detail in Chapter 5. Through the use of symbolic language, the dying sometimes indicate knowledge of the timing of their passing. Doug, a former athlete and coach, suffered from lymphoma. While experiencing NDA, he drew a diagram of a football play with circles for the two teams. One circle bore Doug's initials with an arrow pointing out of bounds and labeled, "Out of the game by noon on Sunday." Just before noon on Sunday, Doug passed away peacefully (Callanan and Kelley 1997, pp.113–15). This account illustrates that important communication was available that could have been easily overlooked by the family. But in understanding the latent message of Doug, loved ones were not only able to be more prepared for death to occur, but were also given the opportunity to acknowledge assertiveness and choice that some individuals seem to have been given while dying.

There are many methods besides speech that the dying may use to communicate their needs metaphorically. Patients who are no longer able to speak, write a note, or even lift a finger need special attention, because they too may want to express their thoughts either directly or symbolically. Many people can learn to draw their concerns or write with a pencil in their mouth. Children, for instance, may "speak" non-verbal symbolic language via their drawings and in their imaginative play. In fact, documented cases exist where, in their drawings, children show ahead of time when metastases begin to develop, creating greater urgency to be able to read and interpret these drawings for better communication (Kübler-Ross 1997b, pp.39–40).

The words of the dying can be bountiful blessings waiting to be decoded and embraced for spiritual discernment and growth. By dismissing their decipherable messages, we lose final opportunities to connect, experience what is beyond, and be of productive use to our loved ones. It is imperative that the world becomes more educated in the importance of symbolic language, promoting greater sensitivity and communication with the dying.

3

Deathbed Visions

Accounts of deathbed visions (DBV) have always been related and documented within many diverse cultures. A DBV is an otherworldly experience that occurs before the death of a person, and on rare occasions can be witnessed by those in attendance. It can take place moments, weeks, or months before the actual death occurs.

A typical DBV experienced by a dying individual is usually invisible to others nearby. According to current research, most visions are of departed loved ones, often radiating or surrounded by an intense light. This deceased person is almost always someone who was close to the dying person such as a parent, child, sibling, or spouse, but can often be religious figures such as the Virgin Mary, angels, Buddha, saints, Krishna, Jesus, or Yama (the Hindu god of death) among others. The figure is always one that is relevant to the dying person, correlating to their own personal belief system. Many dying people report that the purpose of these visits is to ease transition to the other side, and as a result, there is less fear of death and greater inner peace. Whether from this physical existence or from a spiritual plane, love seems to be a common motivation. As author Elizabeth Kübler-Ross states:

> In general, the people who are waiting for us on the other side are the ones who loved us the most. You always meet those people first... I never encountered a Protestant child who saw the Virgin Mary in his last minutes, yet she was perceived by many Catholic children. You are simply received by those who meant the most to you. (Kübler-Ross 1991, p.15)

For centuries, the dying experience has been documented by various cultures, recognizing mystical experiences, altered states of consciousness, and DBV. Strong similarities have been noted among DBVs in contrasting countries, societies, and religions. Jewish Hasidic literature has numerous accounts describing the DBVs of famous rabbis. Rabbi Shmelke, one hour before he died, saw his deceased father, Rabbi Moshe Leib, standing next to him, as well as his deceased teacher, Rabbi Mikhal (Wills-Brandon 2006). Pansa's sister lay dying in her native country of India. Pansa witnessed her sister suddenly shouting and screaming, saying, "I don't want to go with you two." When asked what had happened, the sister said that there were two people in white cloth that had come to take her away, and she was fighting them. They said that they would come again to get her later (Long and Long 2006).

Astronomer Camille Flammarion approached the concept of visitations from the dead in his three-volume work, *Death and its Mystery* (1921–23). Though DBV were mentioned in literature and biographies, the first book generally recognized in scientific circles was *Death-Bed Visions: The Psychical Experiences of the Dying*, written in 1926 by physics professor Sir William Barrett of the Dublin Royal College of Science. This small work was basically a compilation of cases Barrett had gathered, but was never completed due to the author's own death. The most extensive work in this field was performed by psychologists Karlis Osis and Erlendur Haraldsson who collected over 1000 DBV accounts from both the United States and India. Their research was limited to unsedated patients who experienced visions while their minds were clear a few hours before death ensued (Osis and Haraldsson 1977, pp.15–19).

The evidence collected by Osis and Haraldsson was impressive. Of 1318 apparitions documented, 90 percent referred to visits from deceased close family members or friends. Both male and female patients experienced the same number of mother and father visions. In a controlled sample of 100 cases, two-thirds contained the theme of other-worldly matters, with images of heaven being cited most frequently. Sixteen percent reported gardens and landscapes with strong colors, brilliant beauty, and intense light. Just as mystics over the centuries have attempted to convey, light was repeatedly mentioned in relation to the envisioned place. Visions did not seem to be affected by the patient's personal involvement in religion or lack thereof. Analyses indicated that most cases of apparitions could not be attributed to medical factors such as drugs, hallucinogenic disease, hallucinogenic factors in a patient's history, or high temperature. DBVs appeared to occur in people regardless of differences in sex, age, religion, and education. A large majority of apparitions were lifelike, coherent, attentive to the death experience, and offered a message of an afterlife that should be chosen by the dying to embrace (Osis and Haraldsson 1977, pp.27, 30, 78, 102).

A common behavior of the dying that can occur during a DBV is "the stare," a transfixed gaze where their eyes are fixated on the ceiling and seem to be following a moving object. The patient may reach out to touch what they are perceiving, and/or carry on a conversation with the unseen while exhibiting this strange, wide-eyed expression toward the ceiling. It appears that the statements of those who do speak while exhibiting this behavior suggest that the silent are sometimes viewing and concentrating on deceased loved ones or religious images, but for some reason are unable to express it. Some patients may not openly discuss what they witness for fear of being labeled "crazy." Concern for loved ones motivates many dying patients to avoid sharing their DBVs so that those nearby will not experience distress (Wills-Brandon 2000, pp.92–7, 173). But many of the dying cite a loss of words to express their experience adequately, and some may act as if it is exclusive information for only the selected. Indeed, one man, after sharing that he had seen angels, refused to tell more, saying, "I'm not at liberty to share that information with you" (Kessler 2000, p.58).

Often reported by witnesses are the words "beauty" and "beautiful" that the dying use to describe what they alone were seeing. Well-known author Elizabeth Barrett Browning said just before she died, "Beautiful." Thirty-two-year-old Bobby's parting words were, "I can see the light down the road and it's beautiful!" Three-and-a-half-year-old Lilly, while on her deathbed, told her mother, "Don't worry, Mother, it is very beautiful, and there are angels around me." In his final moments, the nineteenth-century American evangelist Dwight L. Moody said, "I have been beyond the gates. God is calling... It is beautiful"

(Barrett 1926, pp.5, 10). At his death in 1931, the famous American inventor Thomas Edison was reported to have said these final words: "It is very beautiful over there."

When a deceased loved one appears to the dying in a DBV, he or she will be in a state of physical well-being, with the body completely restored regardless of the death circumstances. George Gallup Jr., in his work, *Adventures in Immortality*, told the story of evangelist Billy Graham and his experience with his grandmother the day she passed on. Although she had been extremely weak, she sat up in bed and suddenly announced that she could see her deceased husband, Ben. His death had taken place during the Civil War, when he lost an eye and a leg during a battle. Right before her death, the grandmother said, "There is Ben, and he has both of his eyes and both of his legs!" (Gallup with Proctor 1982, p.11). Mrs. Shepherd Nunn, wife of an English vicar, told the story of an old man named John George who was being attended to by his wife at his deathbed. Sadly, the same year their son, Tom, had been killed on the railroad on which he worked. Before his passing, he told his wife, "Why, Mother, here is Tom, and he is all right, no marks on him. Oh, he looks fine" (Barrett 1926, p.9). Only deceased loved ones are perceived in DBV, as opposed to those still present on earth. Interestingly, there are numerous documented cases, discussed later in this chapter, where the dying reported seeing a loved one who had recently died. However, the patient had not been informed of the loved one's death.

DBV must be basically experienced and/or observed. Therefore, in order to grasp their depth and fullness, the phenomenon of DBVs is best understood on a case-by-case basis (Osis and Haraldsson 1977, p.32). But once examined individually, however, common themes tend to reoccur. In addition to apparitions of deceased loved ones, divine beings seem to be predominant figures in DBVs, and are typically accepted freely by the dying. In 1916, Ruth Anne Dodge, wife of Civil War general Granville Dodge, had a vision of an approaching boat. In the prow was an angel who carried a small bowl under her arm, while extending the other arm toward Ruth Anne. The angel invited her to "partake of the water flowing from the vessel." Two more times the angel visited, saying, "Drink. I bring you both a promise and a blessing." Following the third visit, Ruth Anne told her two daughters that she had drunk of the water and experienced the feeling of being "transformed into a new and glorious being." She died soon thereafter. The daughters honored the DBV by commissioning a statue that would signify their mother's angel standing in the boat, holding the water vessel. It stands today on a bluff near the family home in Council Bluffs, Iowa, a monument to the DBV experience and those who heed the visions of the dying (Wooten-Green and Champlin 2001, pp.81–3).

Belief in a Higher Power is not a prerequisite for a DBV involving a religious figure, or in experiencing serenity and security from the experience. Angela, a 25-year-old melanoma patient in hospice care, demanded that there be no spiritual intervention for her because she was an atheist. One morning she told the nurse that an angel had been sitting in the light by the window the previous night. Although Angela's mother said it was a sign from God, Angela stated, "I don't believe in angels or God, but someone was here with me. Whoever it was loves me and is waiting for me. So it means I won't die alone." Despite her personal spiritual beliefs, Angela's DBV was comforting and lessened her solitary feelings about the death experience (Callanan and Kelley 1997, pp.89–90).

Countless other documentations of comforting religious figures exist. Pediatrician Melvin Morse, in his book, *Closer to the Light*, told the story of his 11-year-old patient named Seth who was dying of lymphoma. As his condition deteriorated and breathing became labored, he asked his bereaved parents to "let him go." He said, "Don't be afraid. I've seen God, angels, and shepherds. I see a white horse." He went on to hold his hand out in front of him and share that he had seen where he was going, and it was beautiful. This vision seemed to provide reassurance and consolation to his family that he was in a better place (Morse with Perry 1990, pp.56–8). Morse also shared the experience of a dying leukemia patient who said that Christ had come to him in a vision, reaching down from above and asking him to come with Him (Morse with Perry 1994, pp.xxiv–xxv).

While maintaining a vigil at the bedside of her dying brother, a woman began to hear soft, serene music and looked around to see if the radio was on. As she turned, a brilliant light completely filled the sick room, and she saw her comatose brother with his eyes open, smiling and raising his arms upward. The woman stated later that "As real as anything I've ever seen, a being of light reached out and took my brother by his wrists and pulled. My brother's spirit popped right out of his physical body." She then saw the being of light and her brother's spirit leave the room through a mistlike archway, and could detect the strong scent of roses (Atwater 2005, p.109).

Stanley Peele was a Bible reader at the University of North Carolina Hospital, and visited an elderly woman who had suffered four debilitating strokes. After he read to her Psalm 63, she asked Peele, "Is that your daughter?" He replied that he saw no one. The woman appeared annoyed and asked again, "Is that your daughter?" When asked if she was seeing angels, she answered yes, with a strong voice and clear eyes, and that it looked like a ten-year-old girl. Interestingly, her pain had disappeared. The vision seemingly provided comfort to both the dying woman and Peele, who now believes the angel accompanies him on his hospital rounds (Peele 2002, pp.1–2).

Visitations can also provide a touch of humor. Judy's dying father frequently complained of little girls chatting. When asked if they were angels, he replied, "I never looked at them, but I know they're girls because it's yakety-yak all the time." A neighbor then reported seeing angels outside the father's house in a tree (Long and Long 2006).

A DBV that included a physical effect was reported by a Christian nurse who was with a 40-year-old patient in India:

> He was unsedated, fully conscious, and had a low temperature. He was a rather religious person and believed in life after death. We expected him to die, and he probably did too, as he was asking us to pray for him. In the room where he was lying, there was a staircase leading to the second floor. Suddenly he exclaimed: "See, the angels are coming down the stairs. The glass has fallen and broken." All of us in the room looked toward the staircase where a drinking glass had been placed on one of the steps. As we looked, we saw the glass break into a thousand pieces without cause. It did not fall, it simply exploded. (Osis and Haraldsson 1977, p.42)

Another repeating theme in many documented DBVs is that of the apparition's intent to take the patient away to a better place. As a result of this powerful spiritual moment, the dying suddenly become eager, excited, and luminous in appearance to those in attendance. Thirty-six-year-old Mrs. Brown was in the final agonizing stages of cancer when her suffering appeared to cease. Her previous facial expression of excruciating pain was replaced with radiant joy when she raised her hands and said, "Oh, mother dear, you have come to take me home. I am so glad!" (Barrett 1926, p.2). Betty in Australia told of her "Granny" in a medical facility approaching her 107th birthday. While Betty's sister was visiting, Granny shared with her that a man had recently appeared at the foot of her bed, and told her to get ready because he was returning the next day to take her to see her deceased mother. Although the nurse on duty said that Granny was in relatively good health and should continue to live, the next day, Granny died (Atwater 2005, p.59).

A medical worker responded to a research survey with the following story. When a 16-year-old girl emerged from a coma, she appeared to have a clear state of consciousness: " 'I can't get up,' and she opened her eyes. I raised her up a little bit and she said, 'I see him, I see him. I am coming.' She died immediately afterwards with a radiant face, exultant and elated" (Osis and Haraldsson 1977, p.34).

The wife of a dying patient told hospice nurse Kathleen J. Rusnak of a visitation from the other side. Her husband accused her of being rude, saying that his father was sitting over on the sofa, and that she should at least say hello to him. She complied by saying, "Hi, Dad" to the man who had been dead for 20 years, even though she could not see him. Two days later the husband died, stating that his deceased mother came back to take him home with her (Rusnak 2006).

Here are some documented examples of DBVs that I gathered from nursing home staff:

> "One resident (at the home) was looking up toward the ceiling, smiling holding out her hand, then saying, 'There you are, I've been waiting for you.'"

> "My husband's uncle, a minister, heard the angels singing. He said, just listen, they're singing beautifully."

> "I took care of a 107-year-old woman who said she saw angels in her room for a week before her death."

> "I was with my dad when he was dying… He said he saw angels in a big white room. They were inviting him to come in."

> "My sister died two years ago. She spoke about our brother (deceased) holding his hand out to her."

> "I've seen patients staring into the air and reaching out, calling the names of loved ones who were already dead."

The DBVs that are experienced by others who are not dying occur much less frequently according to researchers, but are no less valuable in a spiritual sense. When witnesses perceive a vision related to their dying loved one, many obtain a new sense of relief, interpreting the vision as strong evidence of survival after death. According to Sir William Barrett, there are many authenticated cases on record where people near the deathbed have seen at the moment of death a cloudy form rising from the body, hovering for a time and then passing from the room. A Dean of the Anglican Church, while at his son's bedside, said that just as the boy's breathing ceased, he and his wife saw "something rise as it were from his face like a delicate veil or mist, and slowly pass away" (Barrett 1926, p.2). Sharon was beside her mother as she was dying and reported this experience:

> I looked back at mum and there was a light forming around her, the color is hard to describe but it was like a golden pale lemon color... Then it was completely above her. When I looked at the light above mum I couldn't believe what I was seeing as mum was in the light, floating above her body! Then she moved slowly towards the corner of the room she was reaching for before, and once again stretched out her hand to greet someone, then she was gone. (Long and Long 2006)

Louisa May Alcott, author of *Little Women*, wrote in her diary the witnessing of her sister Beth's death, stating that she and her mother "saw a light mist rise from the body and float up and vanish in the air" (Alcott 1913). Robin, whose husband was dying, was at his deathbed in the final moments along with a priest and a friend who was holding Robin's young son in her arms. As her husband's last breath was taken, all three saw a golden-white light travel in an arc from the husband to explode around the son. It is Robin's belief that the arc was a symbolic act of fatherly love and protection (Atwater 2005, p.96).

Author Kathleen Dowling Singh, in her book, *The Grace in Dying*, tells of a vision in which she perceived the image of the Divine Mother, whose hands, elongated almost in the style of Eastern Art, were gently soothing, back and forth, the worn and damaged body of the one who was dying

(Singh 2000, p.241). Jim Barnett had a near-death experience (NDE) when he was 30, and while unconscious had a vision of a woman with long red hair telling him that he would survive. Years later when his wife Marjorie was dying with cancer, a young red-haired woman, who was the same visitor as years before, entered Marjorie's bedroom. All three talked well into the night, and the woman told Marjorie that she would be waiting for her and that Jim would follow later. Much later in the night, it occurred to Jim that he had had a sister with long red hair who died very young (Sharp and Terbay 1997, pp.28–9).

Challenges as to the veracity of DBVs are many. The most frequent assertion is that while the brain is dying it is randomly expelling from its long-term memory images stored from the past. Author Carla Wills-Brandon defends the existence of DBVs by making several pertinent points. If DBVs are the result of chemical imbalances, oxygen deprivation, neurosis, or wishful thinking, then why are virtually all visions of the deceased, and why are the themes in visions consistent with one another? Random brain firings would bring forth chaotic visions that would be disparate in content. Wills-Brandon also points out that the consistent goal of the subject in the vision is to assist the dying in the transition to another realm of existence. The common pattern is a pointed intent specifically directed in the vision, which is not in keeping with the random firing of the brain (Wills-Brandon 2000, pp.162–4).

Melvin Morse addressed the question of whether the human brain creates its visionary experiences as opposed to receiving them telepathically in an area of the brain where physical and spiritual worlds meet:

> After examining thousands of case studies, and
> even after having had a death-related vision of my
> own, I can say without a doubt that the brain both
> creates visionary experiences and detects them.
> There seems to be a huge area of the brain that is
> devoted to having just such experiences. Just as we
> have a region of our brain devoted to speech and
> one that helps us regain our balance when we trip
> and almost fall, we have an area that is devoted to
> communication with the mystical. It functions as a
> sort of sixth sense. In short it is the "God sensor."
> (Morse with Perry 1994, p.71)

The primary question still arises: how can these frequent
occurrences be verified scientifically? The psychiatric community could easily note that thousands of people all over
the world have common types of "hallucinations" before
dying, specifically the recognition of well-loved family
members or friends who had preceded them in death. Elizabeth Kübler-Ross believed that one possible way to study
this phenomena was to be with dying children after family
accidents. During times when families traveled together,
such as Labor Day or the Fourth of July, head-on collisions
often resulted in the death of some family members and the
hospitalization of injured survivors. She was able to
document consistently that while she was sitting with criti-
cally injured children who had not been told of the deaths of
any relatives, many children were aware of the presence of
their deceased relatives (Kübler-Ross 1991, p.53).

There are many reported instances where a dying patient
had not been informed or aware of a family member's death,
and yet were greeted by them in a visitation. A hit-and-run
driver struck a Native American woman on a highway.
When a stranger stopped his car to help her, she told him

that if he was ever near the Indian reservation 700 miles away where her mother lived, to give her mother a message: she was okay and very happy because she was already together with her father. The woman then died in the stranger's arms. He was so overcome by the experience that he drove the 700 miles to visit the woman's mother. When he reached the reservation, he learned that the mother's husband, the woman's father, had died of a coronary one hour before the hit-and-run accident (Kübler-Ross 1991, pp.53–5).

Is it essential to have a scientific explanation for why DBVs occur? When all is said and done, the end result seems to be the most effective gauge for their existence, and "By their fruits ye shall know them" could easily be the barometer of authentication. DBVs can provide a sense of peace, security, and reassurance to both the dying and their loved ones. Spiritual calm and comfort can emerge for all following a DBV experience. A Mrs. Campbell said after the death of her husband, "I am very glad my dear husband saw our son before he died... I shall now be able to think of them as always together and happy. And when I receive my summons I know that they will both come for me" (Barrett 1926, p.4). A certain Mrs. Dyer's 14-year-old son, Charles, was slowly dying of consumption in Brimfield, Herefordshire, England. One morning, she found him sitting up in bed, happily stating that a nice, elderly man had come for him with arms outstretched. Charles told his mother not to worry, and then died with a joyful smile on his face. Mrs. Nunn, a friend of Mrs. Dyer, described the mother's reaction: "His mother was full of ecstasy, and came down to the Vicarage that same morning to tell me of it. The impression this experience made upon her has continued to the present day, and has influenced her life for the better" (Barrett 1926, p.9).

What if a dying person does not ever experience a DBV? Does that mean that their spirituality is shaky, or non-existent? Absolutely not, in my opinion. Having a DBV or visitation from a religious figure or loved one is not a barometer of personal spiritual health, nor a dramatic message from the other side that something is amiss. Some individuals simply have them and others don't; there is no way to determine why, except to believe that perhaps it was supposed to happen for a reason. Other factors to consider are that those near the dying may not be aware that a vision has taken place because the dying may not share it, and that communications to the dying may occur during thought processes and/or dreams on different levels of consciousness. Perhaps witnesses are not always supposed to be privy to the occurrence of a DBV or other communication from another level of existence.

Many people view death as a lonely experience, and fear that they or a loved one will die alone. The spiritual beings that emerge during a DBV can provide assurance that no one is alone and that there will be companions on the journey to yet another chapter of life (Callanan and Kelley 1997, p.97). For many individuals, the DBV experience is valid proof of survival after death. A sense of perpetual life is promoted when deceased relatives and friends return to escort the dying to another stage of existence. Their appearance is a wondrous and bountiful blessing, often a "family affair." Visions of a religious figure or place so beautiful that it cannot be adequately described are spiritual gifts of joy and anticipation, promoting the assurance that there is more to life than what we deal with in the here and now. From my own perspective, God is "doing His/Her thing," sending us awe-inspiring messages of love and support, and urging us forward on our spiritual journey towards oneness with our Source.

4

Pre-death Dreams

People with terminal illnesses have a lot on their minds. Knowing that they are living their final days on this earth, a variety of issues can weigh heavily on them. What is dying going to be like? What happens to me after I die? Do I need forgiveness and/or reconciliation with someone or something in my life? Are my financial affairs in order? Am I spiritually at peace with myself? Many times these questions as well as their answers can surface through pre-death dreams. By paying close attention to the meanings inherent in their dreams, the dying can find ways of successfully bringing peaceful closure to their earthly existence.

Death is a concept that is with us throughout our lives. Even as children, a fascination as well as fear of death takes root, with the questions about our own demise permanently stored in the bottom shelf of our library of life concerns. Dreams can provide a clear display of these lifelong curiosities and fears. For the dying, pre-death dreams can be especially beneficial and therapeutic. Since death is the ultimate ending point for the dreams of the terminally ill, it is no surprise that more pre-death dream accounts have been collected by nursing home staff, hospice workers, and family members than dream researchers. But those in the scientific arena are still aware of the importance of these dreams and potential path for growth they can provide for dying patients – and sometimes even their caregivers (Underwood 2005).

Pre-death dreams can take place with consistent regularity among the terminally ill, often occurring over the course of several consecutive nights. Since all of us dream throughout our lives, pre-death dreams are both a familiar and logical experience for the dying to undergo when they fall asleep. The content of the pre-death dream usually is dependent on where the patient is physically, emotionally, and spiritually at that particular time. It can reflect distinctive shifts and forward movement in the self-awareness of the dying, illustrating growth and preparation for death (Bulkeley and Bulkley 2005, pp.23, 28–9, 140). Edgar Cayce, the twentieth-century American psychic, stated the spiritual importance of dreams in a reading: "It is the natural – it is nature – it is God's activity. His associations with man. His desire to make for man a way for an understanding" (Frejer 1999, p.100).

Countless documentations exist that bear the recurring theme of death premonition, often with the dreamer actually learning the accurate time of his or her passing from a previously deceased loved one or friend. Lawyer Gaetan Re David confided in a friend that he never dreamed of his deceased mother in all of his 41 years. But the previous night he dreamed of her approaching him with outstretched arms, summoning him forth. Re David believed, based on the dream, that his death was quite near; a few days afterward, he died (Flammarion 1922, p.87). In 1913, author Camille Flammarion received the following account from a Madame Suzanne Bonnefoy in Cherbourg, France, concerning the death of a friend:

> The servant of Monsieur Féron, an attorney... came to tell me of the sudden death of his master, which had occurred ten hours before... Very much moved, I ran to offer my services to his wife Madame Féron... "And to think," she cried on seeing me, "that for a month he has repeated constantly that he would never see the end of January. Just lately, he had been to the burial of one of his friends, and had had, on the following night, a very strange dream, in which his friend had appeared and had said to him: 'On such a day you will come and join me.'" ... Monsieur Féron was taken suddenly ill in the street and died in half an hour, carried off by a heart attack. (Flammarion 1921 p.166)

Monsieur Féron died on January 18, proving true both his belief and the dream prophecy that he would not see the end of the month. A Dr. Lyon in Dublin, Ireland reported a similar incident:

> The late Mrs. Dorcas Norris had told me several times that Mrs. Elisa Carleton (a friend) had appeared to her in a dream, and had promised to appear to her one last time, twenty-four hours before her death. The night that preceeded her death she announced that the warning for which she had waited for fifty-six years had been given her, and that she would die on the following night, a thing that happened. (Flammarion 1922, p.91)

The theme of death preparation in dreams need not be experienced only by those nearing death in a matter of a few days. A young woman in her late twenties was killed outside Jackpot, Nevada, in an early morning car pile-up. Interestingly, several of her family members later stated that she was aware of her coming death, and even knew how it would happen and when, due to a recurring dream that had begun six months earlier. Relatives had noticed that she had been telling people around her what to expect to happen, and had been getting her personal affairs in order (Atwater 2005, pp.12–13).

Dreaming is normally thought of as a sleep phenomenon. There is, however, another avenue for dreaming to take place: waking dreams. Waking dreams are those experiences that manifest themselves in the twilight of consciousness, and are neither daydreams nor hallucinations. This time of rest has also been termed an intermediary state, or half-dream, where the dreamer is aware of consciously participating in the dream, and images are recorded and remembered (Watkins 1984, pp.vi, 14). The following case of Frank illustrates not only a waking dream, but also a pre-death dream experienced by the family member of a person dying. Frank had a young son who was diagnosed with cancer, and weeks before his passing, Frank experienced a dream while seemingly awake in his bed, finding himself in the family room existing as two eyes only. Across the room his deceased father stood with his arm around the ill son (his grandson). The deceased father told Frank that the boy would not make it but to try not to worry. Everything would work out and he would be with him when the time of death came. A few weeks after the dream, the son did succumb to his cancer (Atwater 2005, pp.58–9).

Repeating experiences in both sleeping dreams and waking dreams can often urge the dreamer to examine metaphysical questions never considered before (Van de Castle 1994, p.xxv). For the dying, both forms of dreaming may occur and promote a newfound realization and gravity to the nature of all dream experiences. It is no surprise that a dying person, lying immobile day after day, would have ample opportunity to ponder the nature of reality and re-evaluate life experiences in either a state of deep sleep or while partially asleep.

Historical documentations of pre-death dreams exist from differing religions and diverse cultures, from India to China to Ancient Greece (Underwood 2005). Dreams were considered to be primarily spiritual in nature during ancient times, and were often interpreted as messages, warnings, or prophecies from the gods. Belief in the afterlife possibly began based on dreams, because deceased persons were often seen in the dreams as they once were in life. In Ancient Greece, the common belief was that the gods came through the keyhole of the dreamer's bedroom door and stood beside the bed. During sleep, the dreamer then had the option of leaving the physical body and traveling with the gods. In India, it was believed that if the sleeping person were to be awakened suddenly before returning to the body, the person would die. The Ancient Chinese believed that their spiritual soul, or *hun*, could travel during sleep and also converse with the dead (Van de Castle 1994, pp.41, 57, 60).

Dreams have been referred to for centuries as an opening into an ethereal world, a domain that functions counter to what we experience on earth (Wills-Brandon 2000, p.129). Cultures of the world contain accounts throughout their history of intense dreams where the recently deceased return to earth offering guidance, support, and/or warning. The reoccurrence of these visitation dreams cross-culturally presents one of the most powerful findings of anthropological dream research, and underscores the basic connection between death and dreaming.

An enormous amount of evidence from both anthropology and history supports the concept that dreams offer a universal means of accessing and becoming more intimate with the sacred, a repeating dream theme for the dying. Many dream incubation practices can be found in the belief systems and spiritual traditions of the world, such as Native American, African healing rituals, and Siberian shamanic travels. All hope to reach an intimate interaction between the dreamer and a higher power (Bulkeley and Bulkley 2005, pp.18, 26, 139). Death has always commanded extensive attention in Buddhism, since Buddha's awareness of death promoted his realization of the uselessness of worldly pleasures. Tibetan Buddhist literature states that an interlude of clear light such as the one that approaches at the point of death can be experienced at the moment of falling into the sleep state (Powers 1995, pp.3–4).

Clinical literature offers an abundance of data supporting the idea that dreams contain significant issues from people's lives in the form of metaphors and analogies (Reed 2006). An individual cannot choose to control dreams totally. One's dream, however, can illustrate that nature prepares one for death, and through the use of both archetypal and personal symbols, the perception of an issue and the response of the dreamer are articulated. When the dreams of older people have been analyzed, numerous dream symbols appear that seem to psychically prepare the dreamer for impending death. Symbols can appear that employ a wealth of mythical images, and can reflect the teaching of the religion or spirituality of the individual about the afterlife. These universal as well as personal structures, according to psychologist Carl Jung, are more prevalent during times of crises and can lead to completion and wholeness. Jung stressed that individuation, or the desire for wholeness, was the primary motivator of human personality, and viewed dreams as a vital form of support and direction to self-actualization (Jung 1975, pp.196, 245). Interestingly, in his last articulated dream before his death, Jung saw a large round stone engraved with the words, "And this shall be a sign unto you of Wholeness and Oneness" (Van der Post 1975, p.174). Perhaps he was perceiving his own life's work as full and inclusive, and the dream articulated this. Yet another interpretation could be that he was about to become whole and one with the Source from which he came.

Ellen had endured an addicted mother who used and abused her. Although Ellen had worked on the issue in psychotherapy, when her death became imminent, hidden incidents were finally being disclosed and glaring omissions exposed as if she were cleaning house within. Near the end, Ellen began to dream of her mother in a new way, in dreams that portrayed the two women as merely being together, without the abuse and pain. Ellen, a New York City native, told of a dream where she was living in a wonderful apartment building, the kind she would never have been able to afford. Her mother was there and ecstatic to see her, telling her that the apartment next to hers was available whenever Ellen was ready to move in. Ellen interpreted the apartment and potential living situation with her mother as her vision of heaven (Guenther 1995, p.85). Although Ellen had been scarred from her mother's cruelty and abandonment, the dream articulated that out of her brokenness she gained the ability to forgive and achieve inner healing before death.

There are several repeating metaphorical themes that surface in pre-death dreams. One that often occurs not only in the language and visions of the dying, but also in dreams, is that of traveling on a journey. This theme can illustrate the powerful influence dreams can have in terms of the dying person's re-examination and analysis of the individual's life story (Bulkeley and Bulkley 2005, p.8). The imagery experienced by the dying in pre-death dreams often pertains to travel: paths, ladders, trains, rivers, bridges, gates, and stairs, for example. The dreams may contain actions such as moving to another home, shifting from one place to another, and traveling forward, which enable the dying to prepare for what is to come by mentally grasping the awesome shift of transformation ahead. Yet the imagery is still largely personal, addressing the person in the context of his or her life, promoting a supportive and joyful, intimate expectation. A retired merchant marine captain named Charles Rasmussen was dying of cancer and was consumed with fear until he had the following dream:

> I am sailing again at night in uncharted waters and the old sense of adventure comes back. I feel the tingle of excitement again, of pushing through the waves in the vast, dark, empty sea but knowing somehow I am right on course. And strangely enough, I'm not afraid to die anymore. In fact, I feel ready to go, more so every day. (Bulkeley and Bulkley 2005, p.3)

A hospice worker told dream authority Robert L. Van de Castle of recurring pre-death dreams experienced by a woman dying of cancer. She was on the bank of a river and could see a beckoning hand on the other side. Each time she dreamed this, the width of the river shrank, until a few days before her death it had narrowed to a spring, which she could easily step across (Van de Castle 1994, pp.355–6). For the dying woman, the river may have symbolized life and movement to another dimension of existence, similar to the River Styx, the mythological river of death.

Marie Von Franz, who worked with Carl Jung for over 30 years, documented hundreds of pre-death dreams containing travel as a motif. An elderly woman dreamed this shortly before her passing: "I have packed two suitcases, one with my working clothes, the other, a trans-Europe suitcase, with my jewelry, my diaries and my photos. The first is for the mainland, the other for America" ("Jenseits des Todes" by Christa Meves, cited in Von Franz 1987, p.64.) One interpretation could be that she was not going to be able to take along her everyday possessions (working clothes) to the afterlife, but could still take her inner psychic valuables.

Another theme frequently transpiring in the dreams of the dying is that of life continuing in a new plane of existence. Obviously, the patient's spiritual beliefs can play a prominent role in whether death will be anticipated joyously, as an unpleasant compulsory event for attaining life beyond what is experienced on earth, or as the final ending. But when an evaluation of spiritual beliefs is brought forward at this transitory time, a patient has the opportunity to encounter a deeper level of being and explore humanity's relationship to possibly an unseen Higher Power (Von Franz 1987, pp.357–8, 462) In the following dream of Suzanne, an elderly woman suffering the final stages of terminal disease, the light motif occurs, a frequent image in pre-death dreams, and movement is subtle yet dramatic in the dream's content, suggestive of a shift in existence:

> She sees a candle lit on the windowsill of the
> hospital room and finds that the candle suddenly
> goes out. Fear and anxiety ensue as the darkness
> envelops her. Suddenly, the candle lights on the
> other side of the window and she awakens.

That same day Suzanne died, "completely at peace" (Fourtier 1972, p.1).

After a series of debilitating strokes, Katy's 80-year-old father Ed moved into hospice care. She gently suggested that he pay attention to his dreams. In one dream he discovered that his old clothes were "all twisted up" and he wanted care-givers to dress him in new clothes. The reason was that he wanted to look his best for a trip he was going to take on the aircraft, the Concorde. This scenario seemed to reflect his lack of need for the physical body and coming change to a new realm of existence. A series of dreams followed where Ed was happily doing new work on an "angel machine," with the specific task of combing out the feathers. Near the end, Katy noticed that her father slipped into waking dreams frequently, and moved between two levels of consciousness. After his death, Katy shared that she believed dreaming was a vehicle for Ed to travel to the other side, and to grasp the fact that there is a life of fun on the "other side" (Moss 2003).

Pre-death dreams can illustrate that all of humanity on earth may be part of a unitive wholeness, no matter what the individual's faith or culture. Salah, a Muslim woman who was dying of pancreatic cancer, shared a pre-death dream with her son, Ammar, a few days before her death. She dreamed that she had died, and was in a dark, black place experiencing pain and struggle. Though frightened, she sensed that she must go on. At that point, light enveloped her and Allah was there. She was able to see eternity, a place of peace and no suffering. After recognizing her deceased husband there in a healthy state, she knew the answers to all questions and felt whole and complete (Sharp and Terbay 1997, pp.15–16). Salah's dream supports the theory that pre-death dreams cross religious and cultural boundaries, and that those differences are of no consequence. No matter whether it be Allah, God, Buddha, or others, all of humanity through various religious systems is able to be aware of existence within a larger creation.

Archetypal motifs are common in many pre-death dreams. The course of death can be anticipated by the image of a narrow, dark birth passage. A 74-year-old woman dying of metastatic cancer experienced the birth theme in a dream two weeks before her death. The day before she had been very sick, yet attempted to put her affairs in order. Painful stomach cramps began at that point, then she dreamed:

> She was lying across the opening of a cement pipe about one meter wide, whose upper edge pressed painfully against her stomach. The pipe itself was stuck into the earth. She knew that she had to emerge from it head first and intact into another land. (Von Franz 1987, pp.56–7)

Marie Von Franz interpreted the pipe as the birth passage into another plane of life, and the dreamer was to travel through it head first like an infant when it is born. But the patient had chosen for the moment to lie across it, since she was still involved with her worldly affairs and resistant to the "dark passage" of death. To be reborn would be leaving the old and entering the new.

Margie, preparing for death at home, dreamed that she was walking home from a dance dejectedly, because she was never asked by anyone to dance. As she approached the house, her father appeared and gave her a loving hug. They then walked home arm in arm. Following the dream, Margie no longer feared death. Her symbols seemed to reflect her Midwestern Protestant upbringing accurately, where "home" could be a heavenly, safe, and loving place, and "father" could represent God.

Margie's dream could also be interpreted as one containing a guide, a person such as her father, whose presence evokes guidance, loving care, and reliability. Guides frequently manifest in pre-death dreams, taking the form of a deity, heavenly being, unfamiliar person, or individual previously known on earth. Scott, a high school sophomore, knew Ryan, a senior who died in a car accident. Later, Scott learned that he had an inoperable brain tumor, which gave him only a few weeks left to live, and expressed sadness that he would never be able to get his driver's license. Days later, he happily told a friend of a dream he had, where his dead schoolmate Ryan was alive and sitting in a red convertible. Ryan offered Scott a ride, which he accepted, and off they drove. Not only does Scott's dream suggest travel and happy anticipation, but also the company of a reassuring guide in the form of Ryan. This remarkable dream, with its upbeat imagery of an open-air convertible in vibrant red, gave Scott a fresh perspective on death; he said before his passing that he was actually excited about where his journey would lead (Bulkeley and Bulkley 2005, pp.59–60, 76–7).

Pre-death dreams have an abundance of knowledge to offer the dying as they ponder the life they've lived, the people and situations they've come in contact with, the actual death event, and what lies beyond. There is something liberating about the dream state: rules of logic are discarded and inhibitions are lowered, making one more open and accepting to alternative ways of thinking and transcendent influences (Martin and Romanowski 1997, p.57). As pressing questions materialize within the dreamer, the content can be reflected clearly and answers freely and comfortingly articulated in dreams. As Robert Van de Castle writes, "There are rewards to be found by paying closer attention to our internal dreamscapes" (Van de Castle 1994, p.9). Twentieth-century dream theorist Medard Boss states, "man's ability to perceive things and other people is grounded in his primary openness. If so, there is no reason why man should not encounter what lies beyond the realm of his sense organs" (Boss 1958, p.184). For the dying, their dreams can bring welcome relief and release from inner and outer discomfort, allowing full expression of the soul.

In the dreams of those who face death, the unconscious seems to be preparing the conscious for what is ahead – a dramatic transformation and continuation of life that the everyday conscious is unable to imagine (Von Franz 1987, p.156). Eighteenth-century philosopher and theologian Emanuel Swedenborg stressed that we are rarely conscious of the *real* world, that of the spiritual. There exists around us a marvelous, unheard, unseen universe (Rhodes 1997, pp.34–5). That mysterious barrier between levels of consciousness may be temporarily breached in dreams, with the seemingly supportive intent of promoting acceptance as death draws closer. My own view of sleep is that it is not only for the purpose of rest and decreased consciousness, but also an opportunity to connect with our spiritual nature and commune with the Divine One. By using what psychologist and dream explorer Henry Reed calls the "letters of the soul," dreams can awaken us to universal awareness (Denwiddie 2003).

Dreams can hold powerful significance for the dying. Family, friends, and caregivers can play a vital, supportive role in the process of pre-death dreams and offer helpful encouragement. Although the dying cannot with assurance cause pre-death dreaming to take place in a constructive manner, one can first broach the subject of dreams and their importance with the patient, and suggest that the dreamer makes a concerted effort to try to remember his or her dreams. Remind them that all they need is an open mind and willingness to discover new insights about themselves. If physically and mentally able, a dream journal can be kept at the bedside to record their experiences, using either a tape recorder or pen and paper. If interested, the patient may be able to express and explore a dream aesthetically through drawing pictures or creating a mandala, an artistically balanced figure that can promote inner awareness. Caregivers and loved ones can ask the patients to share their dreams and what possible implications they hold. Particular attention should be given to any dramatic or recurring dreams, which can vividly express their pressing concerns or needs that need to be addressed for greater serenity (Callanan and Kelley 1997, p.196). Questions and comments can be helpful, but care must be taken in allowing the dreamers to analyze the significance of their own dreams, since each is his or her own expert when it comes to discernment (Bulkeley and Bulkley 2005, pp.135–6). Edgar Cayce once stated: "Interpret them [dreams] in thyself. Not by a dream book, not by what others say, but dreams are presented in symbols, in signs" (Frejer 1999, p.102).

Dreams not only promote an exchange of ideas between a dying person and his or her loved ones, but also offer an opportunity for cherished sharing. During a dream discussion, companionship is offered in a setting where the dying can freely express themselves. Their inner longings and issues can emerge with a sense of safety and confidence through the plot of the dream. Pre-death dreams can function as windows into the spiritual health of the dying, as Florence relayed in sharing her dying mother's dream:

> She dreamed she was in a boat on the river of death, she just wanted to get to the shore and die. These large arms drew her out of the boat and set her on the shore. She saw the brightest sunshine she had ever seen and said that God sang to her all night and put her back in bed for three nights. (Long and Long 2006)

Florence's mother had been in and out of consciousness in the hospital for those three days. But when she awoke from her dream, she stated that she was quite peaceful and no longer feared death.

Pre-death dreams are a dual gift to those who are willing to recognize and affirm them. With physical life on earth approaching closure in its mysterious way, family, friends, and caretakers can do the greatest service to the dying by facilitating in this unique form of communication that allows possibilities of enlightenment within themselves, with each other, and with a Greater Power. By doing so, the potential rewards are a greater sense of relief and relaxation for the coming transformation to another plane. But more importantly, in utilizing the latent messages in pre-death dreams, a person can actually experience inner growth, attaining closer spiritual intimacy with their chosen Higher Power.

5

The Timing of Death

It seems that most people view the time that their death will occur as something that is totally out of their hands. A common belief is that death can have a power of its own, and will steal upon a person, catching everyone unawares. Countless documented accounts contradict this idea. Instead, the theme that surfaces is that many times, depending on the physical condition of the patient and the circumstances of the death, humans can have the ability to actually choose the time in which they will pass from this earthly life.

In choosing the time and conditions of departure, the dying may be illustrating an assertive power, a final exercise of free will. Many individuals, including myself, believe that before a soul enters earthly existence, he or she agrees on what life goals are to be accomplished in order to achieve greater oneness with the Source, or Higher Power, from which the soul came. In choosing the time of death, the dying person, in a final earthly moment, can utilize the will of the soul on a subconscious level. Depending on how well the soul has accomplished its life goals, it may choose to remain on earth until closure is reached with a particular issue or situation, or leave earth if closure has been attained.

On a more conscious level, some patients appear to exercise control over the timing of their deaths to be present for holidays, anniversaries, graduations, births, etc. A Christian priest, Murray L. Trelease, served villages in the Alaskan interior, and became aware of how the dying ones showed a willfulness concerning their deaths. He stated that on many occasions when delivering Communion at Christmas or Easter, the dying person would say that he had been waiting for the priest to come. Once the sacrament was delivered, death would soon occur. Trelease stated that, based on his experiences, the human will can be a factor in determining the time of death (Kübler-Ross 1975, pp.33–7).

It appears that the dying are often preoccupied with dates. A mother in the following account seems to have an intuitive awareness of when she will depart:

> On my last birthday, before she passed, my mom was alive and well. We had decided to spend my birthday shopping. During that shopping trip she told me she would pass on in six months. I said, "How do you know?" She then said to me, "You are not the only one who knows things. I know things too." Six months later, to the day, she did pass to spirit. (Wills-Brandon 2000, p.188)

A study published in the *Journal of the American Medical Association* (JAMA) in 2004 stated that cancer patients are unable to delay their deaths to reach Christmas, Thanksgiving, or their birthdays (Young and Hade 2004). But an article printed that same year in a Columbus, Ohio, newspaper points out that there are many personal stories that contradict the JAMA conclusion. Pauline King, a nurse at Arthur G. James Cancer Hospital in Columbus, stated that she has been a witness to many cases where the patient deliberately postponed death. She shared the particular story of a breast-cancer patient with four children, including a 16-year-old. "She told me, 'I'm not going anywhere until my daughter is 18. When she's 18, she'll keep the family together.' And by golly, she made it. To me, it's mind over matter" (Hohlik, *The Columbus Dispatch* 2004, pp.1–2). While presenting a lecture, Elizabeth Kübler-Ross was once asked how to deal with a seriously ill 14-year-old who kept saying she was going to die when she was 18 years old. The world's foremost expert on death and dying replied, "I would listen to her and believe that she may know more than we do." Kübler-Ross also stated that she knew of innumerable patients who had asked medical staff to call family members, or who wanted to call a favorite nurse to thank her for special kindnesses. Many patients asked a nurse to comb their hair and put a new shirt on, to make them clean and presentable. The patient would then ask to be left alone for a little while and when the nurse returned, the patient had died (Kübler-Ross 1997b, pp.8, 36).

While traveling by car to Yellowstone Park for vacation, Margaret, her husband Frank, and their grandson were hit head-on on the highway. Margaret was killed instantly. Frank was barely alive, with his body partially crushed, and the grandson was also seriously injured. After Frank and the grandson were taken to a hospital, the attending doctor found that the boy had a broken pelvis and would recover. When Frank was told that the boy would live, he drew a sigh of relief and immediately died, at peace with the knowledge that his grandson would survive (Atwater 2005, pp.101–2).

There are countless documentations of the slowly dying being able to forecast the time of their deaths correctly. In my opinion it is quite possible that the Divine is communicating intuitively, informing them of the coming event for an unknown reason. During an in-service (training seminar) that I presented to nursing home staff, a nurse told me of a special patient that she had become close to. On Friday, the nurse bid the patient goodbye, saying that she would see her on Monday. The patient replied, "Honey, I won't be able to talk to you on Monday, as I'm leaving. But I love you." When the nurse arrived at work on Monday, she learned that the patient could no longer speak, and later that day, passed away.

Edgar Cayce, the psychic who has been termed the "American Prophet," stated on New Year's Day, 1945, that he would be buried on January 5, which he was (Crystal 2006). When my mother-in law and her sister were leaving the bedside of their dying father, they told him that they would see him again the next day. He replied, "I won't be here tomorrow. They have come to get me." Indeed, their father passed over before the following day. In *Gifts*, Sharp and Terbay's collection of true stories of the dying, two selections illustrate the uncanny ability to predict. In the first, Dee Baughman shares an experience with her father:

> Daddy had cancer. He looked up at the ceiling and told me to look at the modules being built. He explained that the center of the universe was being recreated and that the modules were part of the scheme. When the modules were completed, his time on earth would be finished and he'd be ready to leave. Later...that night Daddy told me the module would be completed the next day. He died

the next afternoon. (Sharp and Terbay 1997, pp.18–19).

Anne Sharp goes on to tell her own personal story of her mother's correct prediction of when death would take place:

> My mother was diagnosed with a brain tumor. When the neurologist told her she had three to six months to live, she just listened. Later she told a friend that she had six weeks. My mother was right...she lived exactly six weeks. (Sharp and Terbay 1997, p.123)

Numerous well-known people have communicated through their final words an inner knowledge of when their death would take place. Nostradamus (Michel de Notre Dame) was a famous 16th-century prophet who some believe was able to accurately foretell future events. In 1566, his assistant bade him goodnight and said, "Tomorrow, master?" Nostradamus replied, "Tomorrow, I shall no longer be here." When the assistant returned the next day, Nostradamus was found dead near his writing bench where he had left a note, which said: "Upon the return of the Embassy, the King's gift put in place, nothing more will be done. He will have gone to God's nearest relatives, friends, blood brothers, found quite dead near bed and bench." Sobhuza II (1899–1982), the King of Swaziland, called his advisors to a meeting for a discussion of political situations with other African states. He suddenly adjourned the meeting and asked all to leave with the exception of his minister of health. Sobhuza II said to him, "I am going." When the minister asked where, the King smiled, waved goodbye and died. George Herman "Babe" Ruth, one of America's greatest baseball players, was in the hospital with throat cancer in August of 1948 when he told a visitor, "Don't come back tomorrow. I won't be here." That evening a doctor noticed Ruth up out of bed, wandering about his room. The doctor asked where he was going, and Ruth replied, "I'm going over the valley." He went back to bed, fell into a coma and died within the hour.

But it is not only in a person's last words that an innate knowing of death's timing can emerge. With calm and certainty a high school senior told her parents that she would die in a violent accident on the day before she graduated. The day before graduation she and a girlfriend were killed instantly in a car while waiting at an intersection for the light to turn green. Later, a note was discovered among the daughter's belongings. She had written that she knew that she and her best friend would die together in the same accident (Atwater 2005, p.13).

The importance of family and friends seems to be a powerfully motivating factor in when and how the dying choose to leave, and for some, it is important to have certain family members present. Many a death seems to have been postponed, while the dying awaited the arrival of a cherished loved one. Author Maggie Callanan described the death of her father in an interview:

> My father actually chose the moment of his dying. He was very concerned that my mother would be alone with him when he died. I went over to visit them on a weekend and felt very unsettled. I came all the way home to my family but wasn't at ease, something wasn't right... I went back... When I went to see my father the second time, he said, "I'm so glad you're here, now I can lie down." You see, he had been unable to get out of bed for three weeks now. He'd been lying down... He was really

waiting for me to be there so my mother wouldn't be alone. He died that night, in 1981. (Bedard and Callanan 2003)

But at the same time, the dying can exercise the ultimate in selflessness. When they believe that the scene of their death would be painful and/or haunting to their loved ones, the dying may time their deaths so that family and friends will not have to bear witnessing it. Gail, a 34-year-old woman dying of cervical cancer, feared she might die at home and wanted to spare her sons the memory. A hospice nurse named Roberta arrived at Gail's home one day and saw that death was imminent. Gail asked if she was going to die that day, and was told by Roberta that she probably was. Ten minutes before the school bus dropped her sons off at the home, Gail passed away, possibly exercising an altruistic method of making sure her children were not present.

A man named Jim had a 17-year-old son who stated that he didn't want to be left with the memory of his father dying in their home. His mother, however, wanted Jim to remain at the family home as long as possible. One day as death drew quite near, the wife called and requested a quick transfer to the hospice for fear of running out of time. Once the ambulance transported Jim, he expired at the hospice while being wheeled into a room, apparently granting his son's wish (Sharp and Terbay 1997, pp.164–5, 186).

Just as the physical setting can sometimes be chosen by the dying, there are certain individuals who choose to be totally alone, without family, friends, or even general caregivers in the room. Pat, a hospice nurse who took wonderful care of my mother, shared that she had noticed how often deaths took place immediately after a close family member stepped out of the room after sitting with a patient. Indeed, Pat would often experience it herself when she was sitting alone with the dying. Needing to step out to go to the restroom or get a quick break, she would always try to leave when the patient appeared stable. And many times, her exit would be all it took for the patient to die. Pat firmly believed that some individuals want to be alone for death to take place, and simply wait for the opportunity to present itself. Pat noted that often, it is people with private, retiring personalities who want to die in the same manner that they have functioned on this earth.

Christopher Landon, son of actor Michael Landon, recalled his eight-year-old sister asking her father if he was going to die, and when. Michael replied that he was and that it would probably be the next day. On the following day, he called his family together for a few moments, then asked them to all leave the room. A few minutes later he passed away alone (Kessler 2000, p.115).

An unusual case of sparing pain for a family is the one of James Farmer Sr., Texas's first African-American PhD, and a theologian, preacher, and educator. In May of 1961, he lay dying from cancer when his son and other members of the Student Nonviolent Coordinating Committee (SNCC) joined the Freedom Rides, intending to test the nation's interstate transportation system for discrimination based on race. Farmer Sr. expressed concern that his son would experience violence in either Alabama or Mississippi. Farmer Jr. had given his bus itinerary to his parents, and each day Pearl Farmer would share with her husband where their son was that particular day.

Farmer Jr. later wrote that his mother said that her husband had willed his death to bring his son back before the buses entered Alabama. Upon learning that the following day his son would arrive in that state, Farmer Sr. died. His son quickly returned to Washington, DC that night to be with the family. On the following day, the bus that Farmer Jr. had been on was partially burned by the Ku Klux Klan and later attacked in Birmingham by a mob. All riders either experienced smoke inhalation or were beaten (Beil 1998, pp.1, 6; Raines 1983, p.3).

Did Farmer Sr. deliberately die before his son reached Alabama? Did he have an unexplainable "pipeline" of information from the Divine that informed him of coming danger and violence? I believe that it is possible.

Surprisingly, deliberately postponing death and lingering on earth can be a way of unselfishly helping loved ones. David Kessler recalled an elderly woman who was in a coma for 11 months. When she passed, he questioned the purpose in her lingering for so long. But years later, when meeting her daughter out in public, he found the answer. The daughter noted that before her mother became sick, the family was not very connected and only occasionally even saw one another. The coma, however, made them a closer family. Perhaps the elderly woman viewed her coma as a parting present bestowed on her loved ones (Kessler 2000, p.13).

There are cases that suggest that a dying person chose the time and place in which to die, but there is no clear-cut reason as to why. Nevertheless, the scenario still suggests that the patient is in control when the event took place. Ralph became a widower at 83, and declined offers from his children to live with them. Since his health was good, he remained in his community where he was raised. But at 87, he began to slow down, and as a result, Ralph checked with his children to see if they still wanted him to move in with them, which they did. The day before his move, Ralph had said goodbye to friends and organized his personal papers on the dining room table. The next day, when his daughter arrived to move him, she found him in bed. He had died in his sleep, choosing to prepare for his earthly departure and die in his own home (Colarusso 2005, p.78).

Chaplain Ron Wooten-Green tells the story of Sam, a magician and auto-parts salesman. Sam primarily saw himself as a magician, and frequently entertained in various venues. After fighting cancer, he eventually came to the point of giving up. A friend visited him one day, and Sam requested that the friend come closer to him. "Watch me, watch me real close. You're about to see the greatest act of all." Sam's friend watched, but could see nothing unusual. Finally, he realized that even though Sam was smiling and his eyes were open, he was dead. Sam had illustrated absolute control, with perfect theatrical timing for his final performance (Wooton-Green and Champlin 2001, pp.174–5).

Can everyone control the time in which they die? The element of mystery seems to be present, no matter whether one dies in a sudden car accident, or slowly passes in hospice care due to cancer. There are some who say, "God called him home," or "God needed him more in heaven." There are others who claim that no matter what the nature or timing is of the death, that the final exit was preplanned even before they were born. And there are yet those who state that although God has the final say on when death occurs, due to the nature of human will people will sometimes make bad choices, fouling up their purpose for earthly existence as well as those of others around them. No matter what the personal belief is of an individual, a greater question for all could be, "Does it really matter if you know whether individuals control their exits from earth?" Again, mystery, with all of the sacredness that it holds, surfaces in a variety of belief systems, and presents the opportunity to discuss, argue, plead, etc. with a Greater Power. These personal interactions, regardless of tone or content, are moments when people can ask themselves what they truly believe about life, the afterlife, human will and God's will. From these private examinations can emerge greater clarity of spiritual belief, and for those who claim to have no belief, perhaps a more accepting, open-minded perspective towards the beliefs of others. A more empowering spiritual strength from the Greater Power can blossom within an individual, enabling individuals to grow in their faith and perception of what Creation truly is.

6

Nearing Death Awareness and Near-Death Experience – What's the Difference?

"Near-Death Experience" (NDE) is a term coined by Raymond Moody, in his bestselling 1975 book, *Life After Life* (2001), and refers to an unusual experience reported by those who have had a close brush with death and survived to report subjectively what occurred. People who had NDEs were either throught to be dead or were clinically dead as a result of accidents, illness, suicide attempts, military combat, childbirth, or serious injury. Many of those who have NDEs claim that the term is erroneous; they are certain that what took place was not "near-death" but rather *in death*. Dr. Moody (2005) was able to identify nine basic elements that occur in NDEs. They are:

1. A ringing or buzzing noise occurs while one experiences the sensation of being dead.

2. Intense pain disappears and is replaced by a sense of peace.

3. The dying have the feeling of floating above the body while sensing the ownership of a spiritual body.

4. The experience of traveling through a dark tunnel, followed by an encounter with a brilliant white light.

5. Those that do not experience the tunnel may feel as if they are rising into the universe and viewing the celestial heavens.

6. One is greeted by friends and relatives who have already died, who seem to glow with an inner light.

7. Religious figures appear such as God, Jesus, Buddha, a saint, an angel, etc.

8. The religious figure encourages a life review, where every act on earth is relived. An overwhelming sense of love is present.

9. One is told that they must either stay or return to earth. No matter what the decision is, all are reluctant to return.

Dr. P.M.H. Atwater has determined that there are four particular types of NDEs. Although they contain elements similar to those described by Dr. Moody, the patterns are different from what is seen as the "classical version." Her conclusions have held up through 20 years of interviews and analysis regardless of the age, culture, religion, education, or gender of an individual. Atwater has noticed however, that all four types can exist in varying combinations and exist in a series of episodes. But each NDE is a personally distinctive type that belongs to only one person. The four types are:

1. Initial Experience (also known as "non-experience"). A brief out-of-body episode that is usually experienced by those who need little shake-up in their lives for adjustment in how reality is perceived.

2. Unpleasant or Hell-like Experience (Inner Cleansing and Self-confrontation). A scary void or hellish purgatory is experienced, usually by those who possess feelings of guilt, anger, or fear. These people expect to receive some sort of punishment after death.

3. Pleasant or Heaven-like Experience (Reassurance and Self-validation). Happy reunions take place with those who have previously died, or with a religious figure. Those who experience this believe that life is important and has purpose in the broader context.

4. Transcendent Experience (Expansive Revelations, Alternate Realities). Individuals are exposed to dimensions beyond their comprehension, and great truths are revealed to them.

(Atwater 1995, pp.21–84)

Based on her NDE research as well as her own personal experiences with death, Atwater says that she and countless others have encountered and been bathed in a "light like none other" during NDEs. She states that:

> That light is the very essence, the heart and soul, the all-consuming consummation of ecstatic ecstasy...into the one great brilliance of all that is land, all that ever was and all that ever will be. You know it's God... You know who you are: a child of God, a cell in the greater body, an extension of the One Force... There is One, and you are of the One. One. The light does this to you. (Atwater 2005 p.63)

After undergoing a serious heart attack and being treated in an emergency room, a Minnesota man later shared what seemed to be a short episode, or "initial experience," as Atwater terms it: "I felt I was lifting right out of my body. No cares, no worries, no nothing – just like I was floating. I felt I was above my body and the stretcher about four feet, just floating – a strange feeling" (Atwater 1995, p.21). Usually, the individual is able to view the entire proceedings from above. Following a risky childbirth, a middle-aged woman told this story: "I went into shock and could see everything going on in the room including my own body lying on the table. I could hear everything. It was as though my spirit had left my body, and I was looking down on it" (Gallup with Proctor 1982, p.79).

An early documented case from 1851 also appears to be an example of the "initial experience" that Atwater describes:

> Suddenly my whole life began to unroll before me and I saw the purpose of it. All bitterness was wiped out for I knew the meaning of every event and I saw its place in the pattern. I seemed to view it all impersonally... [He witnessed his doctor attempting to revive him.] My consciousness was growing

more and more acute. It seemed to have expanded beyond the limits of the brain... I was dead. Yet I could think, hear and see more widely than ever before. (Haddock 1851 cited in Crookall 1964, p.86)

Two predominant types of NDEs are typically reported by people: pleasurable NDEs and distressing NDEs. Both kinds of NDEs are usually described as being so real that they were larger than life itself. Frequently taking place are the pleasurable NDEs that contain sensations of peace, love, bliss, and/or joy (IANDS 2006b). Usually while traveling in a bright light offering unconditional love, the NDEr may experience a life review similar to those experiencing NDA. But in contrast to NDA, the NDEr can directly experience the impact of their past words and deeds by assuming the identity of every other person with whom they ever interacted. Positive feelings of self-worth and satisfaction can surface from this profound life review (IANDS 2006a). Describing his NDE, a professor said that he "almost drowned. Time passed slowly, and I could leisurely review my life, friends, foes, etc. – all within the space of a few minutes." Another physician said that he was "swept overboard at sea as a young man but survived. Brief, compressed, apparently unrelated events of my life flashed before me" (Gallup with Proctor 1982, p.34). A 32-year-old housewife had a reunion with a deceased relative in the following NDE:

I was choking – had sugar in my windpipe. First, I struggled for breath and suddenly all pain and panic ceased. All was intensely dark and cool. Someone met me...and guided me as we walked or floated down this long hallway. Just then I began to see the most beautiful, vivid purplish color of radiating light. It was just around a corner, and I couldn't wait to round that corner and see what I knew would be God. I never made that bend because I was revived. There was such an overwhelming feeling of love and brotherhood, such acceptance and total tranquility, total well-being. I believe I was met by my grandfather, who had died well over ten years earlier. (Gallup with Proctor 1982, p.36)

Psychiatrist and author Dr. Elisabeth Kübler-Ross described the most unforgettable NDE case she had ever encountered. A man was to be picked up by his family for a holiday outing. While on their way to get him, the wife, eight children, and two in-laws were hit by a gasoline tanker, burning everyone to death. After the accident, the man quit working and began drinking heavily and using drugs regularly. He had changed from a typical hard-working citizen to a complete bum. Two years passed, and one evening, as he was lying on a dirt road, the man was run over by a big truck. At this moment his family appeared in a glow of light, relaying to him how happy they were in their new place of existence. He made a vow to share with the world what he had experienced as a way of redemption for wasting his life for two years. The man kept his promise and shared his story with an audience Dr. Kübler-Ross was speaking to in California (Kübler-Ross 1991, pp.57–8).

In another instance of connection with deceased loved ones, a 12-year-old child who had an NDE confided to her father that it was such a beautiful experience that she didn't want to return. What made it very special was that she experienced having her brother there in the NDE with her, holding her with great love and tenderness. She then said to her father that the only problem was that she really didn't have a brother. The father then tearfully confessed that she had a brother who died three months before she was born and they had never revealed that to her (Kübler-Ross 1991, p.32).

Kübler-Ross went on to do extensive research for years on NDEs. From all of her work she was unable to find even one case of a person having an out-of-body experience that was ever again afraid to die. Patients not only stated that they experienced the feeling of peace and equanimity, but also that they had a new sense of wholeness. During the typical out-of-body experience, there are no missing body parts, if one had been lost previously, which may explain why many patients resist artificial attempts to bring them back when they are in a more wonderful place (Atwater 1995, p.31).

There is, however, a smaller group who relay distressing NDEs. These troubling experiences are described as evoking feelings of horror, fear, guilt, anger, and/or isolation. Some contain life reviews that create feelings of remorse, regret, and powerlessness to rectify the situation. Other disturbing NDEs are reported as promoting feelings of loneliness, torment, and worthlessness. Scary landscapes appear with threatening evil beings and/or frightened humans in peril. Following these frightening scenes, many people have relayed that they have experienced a dramatic change of heart, asking the Divine to allow a return to earth to make amends. Their request is granted. These reports of surrender to a Higher Power indicated that distressing NDEs became pleasurable and meaningful NDEs.

A 30-year-old Maryland investor was undergoing an operation when he experienced a terrifying NDE: "I felt I was being tricked into death... I was fighting faces unknown to me." A middle-aged Illinois housewife with double pneumonia described her frightening NDE: "I would see huge things coming toward me, like animals with baseball bats" (Gallup with Proctor 1982, pp.58–9).

Howard Storm, an avowed atheist, had an intensely agonizing NDE when suffering from a perforated stomach. He first heard voices asking him to follow them through a dark fog. As they went deeper and deeper, the people became aggressive and antagonistic until finally, Storm was forced into a violent mob, which began pushing and shoving him. Physically degrading acts were performed on him, and they began to tear off portions of his flesh. From within him, Storm heard a voice telling him to pray to God, which he did. This seemed to be the determining moment that allowed him to return to earth. A totally changed man from his NDE, Howard Storm is now a United Church of Christ minister in Cincinnati, Ohio (Storm 2005).

In contrast to instances of unpleasant NDEs, there are many recorded cases that suggest transcendent, ethereal experiences that were beyond human imagination:

> I visited different types of worlds, many with different colored skies. I was shown many varied life forms and civilizations in this universe; some appeared frightening and some quite wondrously beautiful... The feeling of peace was there, and for the first time in my life I felt a powerful and unconditional love entering and surrounding my being. (IANDS 2006c)

> What I "saw" were a few (three or four) what I can only describe as essences, clear in substance shaped like inverted drops...they may have been different vibrations of light and perhaps that is exactly what

spirit is… Another unforgettable thing was the lack
of time and space, i.e. the experience of timeless-
ness and spacelessness. I was at one and the same
time in the "past" (medieval times), "present," and
"what will be." (IANDS 2006d)

Psychiatrist Peter Fenwick of Kings College in London conducted a survey on the NDE in 2006, and received more
than 2000 responses. His results showed that the choice of
religious affiliation played no role for those who believed
that they had brushed with eternity, and that even atheists
described themselves as rising from their bodies and perceiving a powerful light. Fenwick stated: "Indeed, some of
the atheist respondents wrote some really cross letters saying
that they had not wanted this experience." Seventy-six
percent of Fenwick's respondents described stunning landscapes, and 38 percent claimed that they had encountered
well-loved deceased relatives and friends. Fenwick went on
to describe NDE perceptions of the dead similar to those
seen in deathbed visions (DBVs) of NDA:

> The dead tend to be seen in the prime of life, even
> though they may have died ill or damaged by acci-
> dents or in ripe old age. All injuries had been
> healed… Some of our respondents reported
> meeting people whom they did not know were
> dead, but who were later confirmed to have been
> dead at the time of the experience. (UPI 2006)

Of particular note from Fenwick's study was that 72 percent
who had the "core" experience stated they considered themselves now more spiritual, and that their fear of death was
lessened (UPI 2006). Fenwick's work draws important
common parallels between NDEs and Nearing Death

Awareness (NDA): the personal belief system seemingly has no affiliation for those who undergo either NDE or NDA, including those who claim no belief whatsover. In both phenomena, many experiencers stated that they encountered dead loved ones, including those whose death they were unaware of at the time of the experience. All those "greeters" that met the experiencers were whole in body, which is identical to the state of deceased loved ones perceived in DBVs of NDA patients. More importantly, just as NDA patients have related that their fear of death had been lessened following DBVs or some pre-death dreams, those who have had NDEs stated a similar shift following their experiences.

Like the NDA experience, NDEs can take place among those from all walks of life. People of all ages, races, sexes, religions, sexual orientation, those with different levels of education and wealth, atheists, and those with or without mental illness are capable of experiencing an NDE at any point in their lives. Other similarities exist between the two phenomena. Just as the dying in NDA experience little or no pain and feel peaceful or even euphoric, those who have NDEs report that their moment of death was not painful and consisted of feelings of blissful contentment. Individuals in both situations frequently encountered religious figures or deceased loved ones in complete states of health, and even deceased relatives whom they never knew (IANDS 2006a).

Those experiencing NDA occurrences and those who have NDEs both seem to undergo positive spiritual shifts following their experiences. Like many NDA experiencers, those who had experienced NDEs overall had less fear of death following an encounter. In fact, some NDErs were so positive about their brush with death that they happily anticipated passing over permanently! A Midwestern housewife who almost died in an auto accident and encountered a deceased relative, later said, "I no longer have *any* fear of dying and almost envy those who pass on before me. I know where they'll be and how truly wonderful it is to be there." After nearly drowning, a California storekeeper stated, "Before my experience, I was terrified of death. Now, I know that death is a very peaceful feeling" (Gallup with Proctor 1982, pp.95–6).

Though the NDE may appear to be impossible to evaluate scientifically, there was an interesting study conducted with blind patients to determine if what NDErs claim is the product of wishful thinking. Blind patients who had absolutely no light perception were chosen to participate in the study. After experiencing an NDE, the blind were not only able to relay who had come into the room first and had worked on their resuscitation, they also were able to give specific details of the clothing of the people present (Kübler-Ross 1991, p.50).

Both NDA and NDE are human experiences that cannot be easily seen, measured, and tested by science objectively. But that does nothing to negate the value and veracity of the overwhelming volume of documented cases obtained, not including the unknown that are never reported. All remain genuine experiences, that actually do seem to provide physical proof of their existence, and appear to infer that life may continue on another conscious plane after the body dies. The two phenomena, whatever their personal and unique content, beg for the experiencer (and sometimes their witnesses) to stop and reflect on the possible meaning of what occurred and its implications for future spiritual clarity and full existence either on the earth plane or another unknown one.

There are, however, distinct differences between NDE and NDA in the terminally ill. For NDA, there is no sudden shift in physical condition that usually happens before an NDE, such as a car accident or heart attack. The apparent purpose of the two types of experience seems to be in contrast: those experiencing NDA are preparing for death, while the prevailing theme of the NDE seems to be for the individual to learn how to live life better in the future when they return. While some NDEs occur during full consciousness, with the patient alternating between conversing with a deceased person and those present at the bedside, NDEs usually occur when the individual is in a coma or other unresponsive state of limited consciousness (Kircher and Callanan 2003).

What do NDE and NDA mean for humankind? These two distinctly different phenomena share common implications from a spiritual standpoint. Both types of experiences imply that there is no pain or suffering immediately before death, and that calm yet powerful feelings of joy and love may prevail. The influences of NDE and NDA can lessen the fear that humanity currently has of death. NDEs, like NDA, have the potential to transform the lives of individuals dramatically, making existence on this earth more personally valuable and fulfilling. The two phenomena contain elements that support the belief that there is more to reality beyond earth, particularly when death takes place. Both NDA and NDEs are seemingly unusual but frequent episodes of the human experience that reach beyond the confines of what we can perceive.

Many individuals believe that an all-powerful, loving Force seems to be present, subtly guiding with genuine concern and devotion. My personal conviction is that the consistency in the appearances of deceased loved ones in both phenomena suggests that life is eternal, and that all will continue to exist in an unfamiliar but rewarding dimension beyond what we now know. There we may be reunited with those we have loved. Also, every person has a purpose in life, a reason for existing and participating on this earth, and will eventually evaluate his or her effectiveness in how successfully their physical life was lived.

7

How to Respond to Nearing Death Awareness

When family and caregivers are near those who exhibit signs of Nearing Death Awareness (NDA), they may sense that their surroundings have a surreal quality. The entire room and its inhabitants may seem to emit a hallowed essence that can be daunting, yet mesmerizing. It is at these holy moments that humanity appears to glimpse a portal to a glorious and powerful dimension. There is no better time on earth for humans to progress spiritually than when receiving this foretaste of heavenly enchantment. It is my belief that the Divine can reveal itself in the emotions and spiritual experiences of the dying, and also in the responses of those who care for them. Closing interactions with a patient can potentially ease them into a more peaceful death. As a result, all involved have the opportunity to grow spiritually from the sharing of sacred moments.

Caregivers and supporters who commit to being helpers during the journey towards death have been called "midwives to the dying" (Bernard and Schneider 1996, p.4). If you are going to assume this important role, a productive way to prepare is to ground yourself by taking stock of your unique qualities. What personal qualities are assets in this situation? What weaknesses could thwart your efforts? What are your spiritual beliefs? What is your goal for the dying, and is it serving his or her needs, or perhaps also your own? (Callanan and Kelley 1997, p.223). Do you feel physically, emotionally, and spiritually healthy for this experience? Thomas a' Kempis, the author of *The Imitation of Christ*, once said, "Keep peace in your own soul first of all, then you can think about making peace between other people" (1967, p.64). Being with the dying can be a long and exhausting process both physically and emotionally. A time of self-reflection can prove invaluable in preparation for becoming a supportive companion as death nears. Keep your own soul nurtured. Read spiritual material that speaks to you. Meditate or pray. Consider speaking with a spiritual director, a person who meets with you to encourage discovery of the voice of a Higher Power within you. Find your own personal method of nourishing your individuality and sensitivity so that you may be an effective healing presence.

James E. Miller, in his book, *The Art of Being a Healing Presence*, gives this definition:

> Healing presence is the condition of being consciously and compassionately in the present moment with another or with others, believing in and affirming their potential for wholeness, wherever they are in life. (Miller with Cutshall 2001, p.12)

By focusing on being a healing presence, those in attendance to the dying with NDA behaviors are offering invaluable assistance and spiritual companionship.

Your actual physical presence itself can validate the situation and feelings of the patient. You can honor their dignity
and worth by how you look at them, listen, speak, and
touch. Be cognizant of physical barriers in the room and
clear a space around the two of you: a curtain may need to be
drawn, a door closed, a radio turned down, or a TV turned
off. When the dying sense your efforts at intimate interaction, they are more likely to feel more free to be themselves
and to open up for a discussion of inner concerns. Keep your
own life experiences to yourself, and share only if you
believe it will benefit the other person. Release any expectation that you might have regarding what the outcome will be
of your time together, keeping in mind that the dying person
is the only one who can ultimately accomplish greater
understanding (Miller with Cutshall 2001, pp.12, 28, 31,
33, 36, 40, 56–7).

The midwife to the dying must be familiar with the
special communication of those nearing death. People who
are experiencing NDA may:

- seem disoriented or confused

- share that they have spoken with someone
  already deceased

- see places and speak to people who are not
  visible

- tell of seeing bright lights and/or spiritual beings

- talk aloud with someone deceased that they were
  close to, such as a parent, sibling, grandparent, or
  close friend

- make remarks and gestures that seem "out of character"

- describe another place as one of beauty and peace

- be able to relay to others exactly when they will die

- stare or wave at something unseen, make hand gestures, and reach for unseen objects or people.

(Hospice of the Florida Suncoast 2006)

When behaviors such as these occur, never assume that you know exactly what is taking place. There should never be any argument, prejudgment, or denial of what the patient innately sees as true and real. Preaching, problem-solving, and offering disingenuous hope are also inappropriate at this sensitive time (Wooten-Green and Champlin 2001, p.162). Here are examples of undesirable ways to respond verbally to the dying:

"I believe these experiences are just fabrications of the mind."

"I recently read research which suggests that these experiences are only the by-product of a dying brain."

"You have been under tremendous stress, and I really do feel your mind has begun to play tricks on you."

"You (your friend/your relative) didn't actually see, hear or feel that. You are making too much out of this, and I don't believe this is good for you."

"These visions are not of God. They are evil."

> "You are in grief over your loss (or fearful of death).
> During these trying times, we all want to believe in
> such things. I suspect this is just wishful thinking."

Here are some possible oral responses when you are asked,
"Do you believe me?" after hearing accounts of NDA experiences:

> "Yes, I believe you! What a powerful experience.
> Tell me more."

> "It's not important whether or not I believe you.
> This is your experience. Tell me what it has done
> for you."

> "I don't know what to tell you. This is incredible.
> Let me ask around to see if I can find any books or
> resources that might help you better understand
> your experience."

> "It sounds like you have had an exciting, life-trans-
> forming event. You might need to spend some time
> processing this. Though I'm not real familiar with
> such things, I would be more than happy to hook
> you up with someone who is. Are you interested?"

(Wills-Brandon 2000, pp.284, 288)

The topic of death itself should never be brought up to a
patient. One should always wait until the patient broaches
the subject. If he or she wants to discuss fear, one can sit
down and listen and ask what in particular he or she is afraid
of. If he or she expresses feelings of regret, resentment, or
pain, whether physical or spiritual, you can then join in
(Kübler-Ross 1997b, p.7). Let the dying be in the driver's
seat. You can be honest and address their concerns straight-

forwardly, but let them guide and control the conversation. If the patient does not want to talk, know that you are still supporting them in silence. Be cognizant of how physically close they want you to sit next to them, and how much company and discussion they desire. Holding the hand can physically convey that you are engaged, but only if it is comfortable for them. Observe their eyes, which at times can silently express what words cannot. Be aware that their skin can be sensitive, and even gentle stroking can be unpleasant. It is through sensitivity, concerted listening and affirming words that the dying can receive the emotional comfort and support they need.

Listen carefully for symbolic language. If you are a nurse or aide for a dying patient, jot down anything that seems out of the ordinary and discuss it with other caregivers and the family. Any communication attempts or singular behavior of the dying should be documented on the patient's chart. Many nurses fail to do so for fear of appearing peculiar or silly to peers. But this silent reticence prevents effective response to essential needs of the patient. Also, symbolic language can provide insight into the death experience. For instance, if a patient has talked about his or her imminent departure on a train, asking what time the train leaves might even supply the actual time that death will occur (Hascup 2006, pp.1–2). Whatever language patients are using (symbolic or plain) should be the mode of communication used in order to interact with them. If, at some point, you feel that they are ready to put into plain language ideas they have expressed symbolically, you can try to change over. But if the patient does not respond positively and/or begins to use the previous communication method, you should immediately switch back to symbolic language. Also, when a patient uses a symbolic non-verbal language, it can be a powerful signal that he or she is not ready to discuss the topic in plain English, because he or she feels more safe in that passive metaphorical situation (Kübler-Ross 1997b, pp.49–50).

The inference to be drawn from symbolic non-verbal language is not always easy to identify, but should be respected and the method used to express it not tampered with. For example, if a dying child creates a drawing of a bird crying as it flies away from its sad family in the nest, remarks should be only about the bird and its family, not that the crying bird is possibly the patient expressing his or her view of what is happening to him/her. Again, let the dying person be the one in control; when revisiting the drawing, the child might later change to verbal symbolic language, or even to plain language.

People frequently participate in several tasks as they approach death, and the spiritual companion should be familiar with these recurrent themes. The dying may make a conscious effort to undertake a life review, often focusing on key relationships. In doing so, they might search for central topics within their lives, determining what lessons they learned and what contributions they made. Forgiveness and a need for reconciliation may surface as a vital issue to be addressed quickly. Those close to the dying should be notified immediately. There may be an appearance of turning inward, becoming less active, more dependent, and beginning to say goodbye to all that life on this earth entails (Kircher and Callanan 2003).

As these common themes and behaviors surface, the true depth of one's spirituality often comes to the fore. It is at this point that the spiritual care of the dying must be addressed as adequately as their physical care. The private inner realm of the dying person can sometimes seem to be full of pain and darkness during the dying process, and without any spiritual support and/or enrichment, the prospect of death can be overwhelmingly frightening and lonely. If the dying try to communicate their needs and these are ignored or mis-understood, they may exhibit agitated behavior. This may be the case when someone seems to have died in pain – their distress may have not been physical, but emotional or spiri-tual (Hascup 2006, p.2). In turning to a personal belief and a spiritual discipline, it is much easier to move past these tran-sitory moments of doubt, suffering, and confusion into a place of meaning and healing. Even those who claim to have no spiritual foundations can be gently prompted to examine what they do believe about life, often resulting in a letting go of the self into a more soothing, tranquil state. Therefore, one of the most valued services a supportive companion can offer is a subtle reminder of the individual's most valued beliefs, guiding them towards a goal of calm and relaxation (Bernard and Schneider 1996, pp.30, 32, 47).

Despite our best efforts, some will approach dying as a time of horrified struggle and purposelessness, and as poet Dylan Thomas stated, "Do not go gentle into that good night." The term coined by author Michael Kearney for this sometimes volatile sense of hopelessness and need for reconnection with a greater Source is called "soul pain." He defines soul pain as:

> The experience of an individual who has become disconnected and alienated from the deepest and most fundamental aspects of himself or herself. (Kearney 1996, p.65)

This is a particular type of suffering which may be experi-enced by those close to death. For those who choose to be midwives to the dying, the recognition of soul pain is a key skill in order to address the patient's needs adequately. Here are some common characteristics of soul pain indentified by Kearney (1996):

- distinctive vocabulary that conveys distress such as tortured, anguished, or suffering

- physical symptoms manifested that do not respond to forms of treatment that are usually successful

- fear emotionally expressed

- agitated frustration and wanting a way out of the situation

- sense of meaninglessness, hopelessness, emptiness.

When symptoms of soul pain occur, family, friends, and caregivers often call upon a psychologist, hospital/hospice chaplain, or representative of the organized faith that the dying has chosen. Though all of these services can provide valuable help, "untrained" loved ones should not underestimate their own unique, special gifts for the dying in the midst of soul pain. Probably the most important message of spiritual care that can be relayed is the stated or unstated promise, "I will come back; I won't abandon you." Dependability is foremost – if you are supposed to return at four, then return at four, no matter what is going on with you personally (Holder and Aldredge-Clanton 2004, pp.10–15).

A midwife to the dying can also employ a variety of interventions to promote inner healing. Soft music, massage, Reiki (an energy exchange between two people taking place with or without touch), family photo albums, dream discussions, and a prompting of reminiscences and spiritual ideals are easily accessible and comforting modes of soothing a troubled soul. Sometimes the most simple of activities or adjustments in room atmosphere, such as soft candles and subtle air fragrances, if the patient so desires, can make an immeasurable difference and trigger tranquil repose.

Often, soul pain will be directly connected to an oppressive fear of death and the unknown that is about to take place. People who have their own acceptance of death are well-equipped to comfort patients with this apprehension by relaying their own energies of serenity and inner strength. Hospital staff members noticed that whenever an African-American cleaning woman entered a dying patient's room, something positive happened and change would occur. When asked what she was doing to achieve this, she told the sad story of a life of suffering in the ghetto, and how she waited once for hours in a hospital waiting room for a physician to come and treat her three-year-old son. Her child died there in her arms. She said:

> You know, death is not a stranger to me anymore. He's like an old acquaintance and I'm not afraid of him. Once in a while when I walk into the room of some of these dying patients they look so scared that I cannot help but walk over to them and touch them and say, "It's not so terrible." (Kübler-Ross 1997b, p.126)

Having "been there, done that" and, most importantly, accepted suffering and death, this wise and giving woman was a beacon of strength and peace to those suffering from the soul pain of fear and dread.

The eyes have been referred to as "windows to the soul." Pay attention to the eyes of a patient, particularly if one suspects that the patient is experiencing soul pain. Even if the dying person is non-verbal or intubated, the eyes of the individual can express fear, anger, and/or anxiety, and can give silent clues or even answers to the question of what the patient needs. Using a prearranged method of response, such as nodding the head, or one or two eye blinks for yes or no, specific questions such as "Are you scared?" or "Do you need to see someone in particular?" can be asked. Questions that require more than a yes or no can be presented with choices of a, b, c, or d (Kübler-Ross 1997b, p.41). For example, "Do you need to see someone in particular?" can also include (a) your wife, (b) your son, (c) your mother, (d) someone else. If (d) is chosen, begin the process again, with the assistance of close family or friends to help guide the choices.

The quiet, reassuring voice of a loved one can frequently dispel seeming disturbance in the dying. Touching by the placement of a hand under the hand of the dying person seems to allow the calm of comfort along with freedom of movement (Singh 2000, p.245). If requested, something as simple as warmed blankets can make the dying feel surrounded by love and security when circulation slows to body extremities (Boerstler and Kornfeld 1995, p.105). The use of the arts can be effective in processing conflicted emotions: movies, painting, crafts, literature, and journal writing can foster a working-through of turmoil within. Meditation, in a form with which the patient is spiritually at ease, can be profoundly consoling during moments of agitation during soul pain. Meditation has been proven to be extremely helpful in letting go of anger, fear, and grief, allowing surrender to a Higher Power. In this letting go of the preconceptions of the ego, hope and peace can emerge.

Comeditation is a unique and surprisingly accessible method to use, especially when a trusted companion on the journey is available to help the dying relax. Developed by Tibetan lamas to be used when attending to the sick and dying, contemporary adjustments have maintained the basic form but adapted it to individual needs. In their book, *Life to Death: Harmonizing the Transition*, authors Boerstler and Kornfeld define comeditation:

> It is a method by which a person who wishes to relax is aided by a companion who vocalizes specific sounds, approved or chosen by the dying, in exact synchrony with that person's exhalations, and allows the body to completely relax, with consequent release of both physical and mental tension. Physical discomfort and emotional unrest become soothed, through social support and spiritual awareness. (Boerstler and Kornfeld 1995, pp.xiv)

The beauty of the practice of comeditation is that the patient is totally in charge. His or her exhalation is the signal for the companion to say the word cues, some of which may be peace, love, God, hope, or whatever has particular meaning for the dying. Even the ceasing of the comeditation session can be controlled by a prearranged signal, such as a blinking of the eyes or lifting of a finger. A wondrous sense of harmony with all of Creation and the Creator can be fostered through this gentle and restful method, easing physical, emotional, and spiritual pain.

For the individual who is open to alternative techniques for attaining comfort and whose skin is sensitive, the practice of therapeutic touch can be soothing. Without actually "touching" the body, the companion places the hands four to six inches away and asks permission from their chosen Higher Power to bring comfort. The hands, body, and healing presence of a Higher Being seem to relay energy that eases physical discomfort and aids spiritual healing (Bernard and Schneider 1996, p.41).

Imagework, a kind of guided visualization, is yet another easily accessible and non-invasive method that caregivers may employ for processing soul pain and addressing physical pain. Michael Kearney used this method with a 30-year-old man named Sean who suffered a terminal malignancy. Kearney asked Sean to imagine himself in a rowboat on a calm sea. After rowing for a while, Sean imagined getting out of the boat into the water, floating and splashing happily, promoting a sense of peace and contentment in the present. When the boat began to drift, Kearney suggested that Sean imagined that the boat came back to him and he was able to return to safety. In a follow-up discussion of feelings experienced from this guided imagery, Sean was able to unearth inner pain in regard to his deceased father whom he deeply missed. Sean completely controlled this visualization in choices he made and could stop the session at will. Another variation of this technique consists of inviting the patient to close his or her eyes, and asking the imagination for an image of anything that seems to call for reflection at that particular time. Imagework has been shown to lead to physiological changes in medical conditions through entry into the world of imagination. Images can connect with the deep inner experiences and dramatically change the quality of the dying process (Kearney 1996, pp.31–40).

Perhaps the most important thing a family member, friend, or caregiver can do when soul pain surfaces is simply to *listen*. From attentive listening to the words and sounds of the dying, we can actively show that we care about them and what they are experiencing. And in that bond that is created between speaker and listener, a recognition by the dying of an offering of self may emerge and comfort, with an awareness of not being alone in their inner pain. Author and physician Rachel Naomi Remen has said, "The most basic and powerful way to connect to another person is to listen. Just listen. Perhaps the most important thing we ever give each other is our attention… A loving silence often has far more power to heal and to connect than the most well-intentioned words" (Remen 2007, pp.143–144).

If we are to accompany the dying on their journey towards death, we also owe it to them to offer a variety of methods uniquely tailored to the individual that can make the trip as easy as possible. It has been noted that the stages of dying are similar to any change that regularly occurs in our existence, and that death is merely the final stage of growth (Kübler-Ross 1975, p.145). We, as midwives to the dying, should manifest an environment that is conducive to the stages of spiritual transformation as death approaches. By performing even the smallest of gestures for the dying, we are providing an inestimable service that taps into the best that resides within all of us. It is the sharing of ourselves that many people believe is an element of the Divine within us all being manifested through our unselfish actions, thus preparing for the loving hand of the Divine to guide the dying gently back home.

8

The Transpersonal and Nearing Death Awareness

"Transpersonal" refers to an interdisciplinary approach, where the purpose of assimilating scientific, historical, psychological, and spiritual concepts is to create a broader, more inclusive knowing. Here is a larger context that acknowledges multi-layered levels of consciousness that can transcend mere personal identity. It is an expanding and encompassing view of humankind, which addresses body, mind, spirit, and the dimensions of human nature. To put it quite simply, it is looking at life as being more than what we see. If the transpersonal is concerned with what is beyond, it can have distinct connections with death and the afterlife. What does the transpersonal have to do with death? Will it be helpful to know? The answer, in my opinion, is a resounding yes. To begin with, since humanity already has a general per-

ception of death, one must know what the term transpersonal actually means in order to grasp the correlation
between the two.

I was raised in the Presbyterian Church by my mother,
and changed to the Episcopal Church after I married. In my
forties I experienced a strong curiosity about New Age
thinking, and began to immerse myself in reading about
topics such as astrology, reincarnation, channeling,
after-death communication, and so on. The exposure to
these esoteric areas made me review what I had always
believed about Christianity based on what I was instructed
as a child to adhere to in my life. I found that incorporating
transpersonal beliefs into my Christianity was actually quite
easy to do, and expanded as well as matured my personal
faith. Biblical passages that I had previously taken at face
value took on a new, refreshing significance, and were more
valuable and inspirational to me. The passage in Luke 17: 21
took on a greater meaning: "For behold, the kingdom of
God is within you." Where I used to think that this passage
meant that there was the opportunity for God to prevail in
how we conduct our lives, I now interpret it in a more
directly spiritual sense; that we are a part of God and the
Divine resides within us. In Mark 11: 24, Jesus said, "Therefore I tell you, whatever you ask for in prayer, believe that
you have received it, and it will be yours." I now see a correlation between the universal laws of attraction and attention
so popular in esoteric thinking these days, and the concept
that Jesus seemed to be trying to get across: that the Divine
notices our actions and responds positively and abundantly.

I now also believe in the body–mind–spirit connection,
and see a distinct association between spiritual pain and
physical and mental illness. Since learning about the
transpersonal perspective, I have found that my approach to
life has totally changed and now includes a recognition of

the interconnectedness of life. I now view myself, people's situations and puzzling circumstances in life with greater awareness and acceptance. Though I still view such things as poverty and cruelty as negative and repugnant, I now can see that there is sometimes more than meets the eye when superficially awful circumstances such as these present themselves on earth. When such things manifest in our lives, I believe it can be for a distinct purpose, whether it is to teach an important life lesson to someone, or to achieve greater good for humanity. In other words, due to the connectedness of all of life, we as humans are capable of functioning for the good of the plan of a Higher Power, no matter how outwardly repulsive the process. Now, when an unpleasant experience comes across my path, I can ask myself why it occurred and is it possible that a valuable lesson was inherent within that I or someone else could take from it for growth. The same can be said for witnessing death and particularly, the behaviors of Nearing Death Awareness (NDA). From what may seem to be a powerfully sad point in time, one can learn spiritually and encourage others to do the same. The result can be a fresh moment of renewal, when life can be more broadly viewed with the added component of continued life beyond.

The transpersonal does not view death as many in the present Western civilization generally do, as an ending to life. Instead, death is only a portion, a condition in the larger picture of ultimate reality where there is no time, no past, and no future, only eternity (Wilber 1996, p.64). Life is essentially timeless and the essence of humankind is spiritual. This viewpoint can expand rather than conflict with traditional faith-based views, since many contain beliefs of everlasting life and oneness with a Higher Power, who guides the creation on earth. The concept of NDA contains key elements of the transpersonal paradigm, both in behavior and philosophy. The transpersonal recognizes the value of both life and the actions that take place within that life. Just as life's meaning can be therapeutic to humankind, so can the dying and their witnesses find spiritual comfort and even empowerment and growth in recognizing the meaningfulness of the NDA experience. Both ideas recognize that what we daily encounter on earth is only a.portion of the many levels of consciousness, and when NDA behaviors transpire, the one experiencing it is naturally and willingly being transported to another realm of existence. Naturally and willingly, because inherent within these layers lies our essential spiritual core, which exists in a vast linkage within the universe. NDA fundamentally gives us an illustrative glimpse into the transpersonal dimension. Kathleen Dowling Singh sums up the relationship between the transpersonal and NDA:

> Understanding the path to the transpersonal realms is the key to understanding the dying process. A human being is an organism designed to realize Spirit. Transpersonal insight describes the journey of human beings as one that leads, as the river to the ocean, directly back to their source in the Ground of Being. (Singh 2000, p.18)

The transpersonal way of thinking is related to and can easily be found within beliefs of many traditional faiths. Tibetan Buddhism teaches that, beyond the parameters of daily life with its ordinary thinking and physical body, there exist other realities, other states of consciousness. Believers assert that these levels are subtle but powerful, and can never die. The 14th Dalai Lama says that when the physical body dies, "There is continuation. Death involves the grosser level of the body. The subtle body still will be there" (Hayward and Varela 1992, p.121). One cord weaves through all levels of consciousness, even though the states of existence change over time. The Dalai Lama explains: "The self exists in the former lifetime, exists in the lifetime, and will exist in the next lifetime...the continuum of the '*I*' moment by moment extends through the whole process" (Weber 1990, p.238).

Reincarnation is not a prerequisite for owning a transpersonal perspective, though it can be included and is a strongly held belief of Buddhism and Hinduism. The *Bhagavad Gita*, which expresses a desire for spiritual vision, says: "One who has taken his birth is sure to die, and after death one is sure to take birth again" (Prabhupada 1986, p.110). The *Zohar*, an ancient Jewish text of Kabbalah (Jewish mysticism), offers a mystical belief in unseen influences, visionary experiences, and the afterlife:

> It has been taught:
> Happy are the righteous
> For their days are pure and extend to the world that is coming.
> When they leave this world, all their days are sewn together,
> Made into radiant garments for them to wear.
> Arrayed in that garment,
> They are admitted to the world that is coming
> To enjoy its pleasures. (Matt 1983, p.94)

The Islamic faith also addresses the topics of death and rebirth in broad alignment with the transpersonal, as in *The Qur'an*:

> Allah will restore all things to life. How can you disbelieve in Allah? You were without life and he gave you life, then he will cause you to die, then he will restore you to life and then to him will you be made to return. (Khan 1997, p.9)

Many people sense instinctively that there is an unseen, larger consciousness that continues beyond the body. It often occurs that when individuals have been informed they have a terminal illness, their awareness is suddenly affected. From their perceptions of themselves, relationships, and their own spirituality, the journey of the dying becomes less outward and more inward, tapping into their own sources of greater inner strength. Knowledge of the finitude of life seems to push the dying to an intense attention to the soul (Kuhl 2002, p.255). Those in good health who claim to have experienced moments of expanded awareness, such as during meditation or a religious mystical experience, refer to exposure to a level of being beyond physical reality. This may provide an explanation why, as author and philosopher Ken Wilber states, "So many people who consistently practice some form of transpersonal 'therapy' report that they no longer really fear death" (Wilber 1985, p.135). States of dreaming and meditation, for example, offer opportunities to experience transcendental levels beyond current reality. If family, friends, and caregivers become receptive during the dying process to the transpersonal dimension, they open themselves to the possibility of curbing the sense of coming loss. The transpersonal perspective is illustrated by sensitivity, depth, and open-mindedness, and by utilizing these qualities, the experiences during NDA can be viewed as a synchronistic impetus to grasp inner peace and greater understanding (Coberly 2002, pp.116–19).

A key component of the transpersonal perspective is the "Perennial Philosophy," which refers to the one Divine mystic consciousness that is composed of the physical and spiritual realms. The Perennial Philosophy consists of four primary doctrines. First, the world of matter and consciousness is manifested by the Divine, from which all realities have their being. Second, humans can not only infer the Divine by reasoning, but also know of its existence by direct intuitive experiences. Third, human beings are dual in nature; they possess an individual ego as well as a Self, the Divine aspect of Spirit within. Last, the essence of human-kind's purpose on earth is to realize identity with Self and come to full knowledge of the Divine Ground of Being (Huxley 1945, p.vii).

When witnessing behaviors common in NDA experiences, one can perceive a distinct correlation between the manifestations exhibited by the dying and the basic components of the Perennial Philosophy. When the dying present symbolic language, describe visions and visitations, and recount unusual dreams, they are illustrating a direct connection to levels of consciousness that appear closer to the Source from which they came. The content of NDA behaviors often reflects surrender of the personal ego, and in its place a fixation with matters more interior and spiritual. In the gradual release of egoistic thoughts and a strong focus on a more expansive view of existence, the dying begin the fulfillment of their purpose on earth, which is first to recognize the Divine, followed by a belief that their being is a portion of the Divine. As previously discussed in Chapter 4, many dream accounts suggest that the dreamer discovers identity with God, Allah, Buddha, or whoever they believe is their Maker and a part of themselves.

Through a transformation in consciousness during the dying process, integration and growth occur as one begins to relate to his or her true self. Though once fiercely resisted, openness occurs and along with it a recognition of one's holy aspect, or Ground of Being, allowing a vehicle for Spirit, or Divine Love. Love is then all that remains when all else is discarded and the shift into transpersonal levels of awareness has taken place. Love remains, as a quality of the Ground of Being itself, and is the final element of life (Singh 2000, pp.70, 80, 239).

At the moment of death, many believe that the dying interact, reincarnate, or remerge with their Source from whence they came in a transcendent moment of peace and wonder. For those who witness this transition into another level of being, new levels of understanding and expression in everyday life can surface and the doorway to deeper existence can open. The opportunity is presented to expand previous ideas about life and what it may contain. Grace is experienced the moment that a connection with Spirit is attained, and fresh realms of possibility open with solemn and awesome revelation (Singh 2000, pp.267, 272). In adopting a transpersonal approach, a person accepts the unusual occurrences that take place as having innate meaning and responds supportively to the needs of the dying. This is an unselfish and reverent time of NDA, when one exhibits an appreciation for the human experience and honors the opportunity to travel in unfamiliar territory where deeper knowledge of what death is really like may await.

9

Connecting the Spiritual Dots

Whether one either experiences or witnesses Nearing Death Awareness (NDA) behavior, the topic of personal spirituality will usually come to the fore. A dying patient, family member, friend, or caregiver may wish to peruse mentally their innermost values and beliefs held dear in their lifetime after unique communications such as symbolic language, visitations, and peculiar dreams have surfaced. But one may ask, what is the next step to help myself or someone else on the soul journey? In other words, what are some specific things that I can do to enable a remembrance, clarification, and possible adjustment of personal spiritual beliefs?

One may want to begin by finding a quiet time for uninterrupted reflection, meditation, or prayer, depending on personal preference. If you are working on your own spiritual refinement, explore what surfaces as you ponder the following questions, as well as other concerns that may arise from them. If instead you are assisting a dying individual who desires spiritual direction, discuss these concepts with them as their physical and/or mental condition allows:

- Do you believe in a Higher Power?

- Do you believe that a Higher Power created you?

- Do you adhere to an organized religion or belief system?

- Is it possible to find the sacred within such areas as nature, art, sports, and relationships, and if so, have you ever experienced it?

- Do you view goodness to be at the core of a Higher Power?

- Have you ever thought that a Higher Power specifically influenced something in your life? If so, what was it?

- If you believe in a Higher Power, do you think that it communicates with you, and if so, how?

- Do you consider yourself in a distinct, ongoing relationship with a Higher Power?

- Have you ever longed for a deeper, more substantial completeness in your life?

- Is pleasing and serving a Higher Power important to you, and if so, how do you go about doing it?

- Do you believe that whatever your shortcomings, there is a neverending love that forgives?

- Do you believe in an afterlife?

- What is your definition of the word *soul*, and do you believe you have one?

- Do you believe that one's soul never dies, but returns to its Source?

- Do you believe that you have experienced a life on earth before this current one?

- Have you ever experienced moments when you felt that you were one with the universe? If so, try to remember what it felt like.

- Have you ever noticed occurrences or situations that seemed to suggest a purposeful pattern? If so, what were they, and how do you explain them?

- If you believe in a Higher Power, do you see yourself as a separate entity, or instead as a part of that greater Whole?

- Do you attempt to live your life in service to others? To a Higher Power? If so, how?

These questions, due to their broad content, should probably be considered in several sittings. If you are spiritually supporting a dying person and he or she gives permission, take notes as the two of you discuss these questions, or if desired, record your conversations. Suggest that the individual privately reflect later on what was discussed. If physically able, the person can then jot down or record any ideas that they want to remember, and at the beginning of the next sitting, the two of you can review together what was said previously, checking to see if any new concepts came forth. If you are doing your own spiritual exploration, write down any thoughts that come to mind with each question in a journal, and return at a later time to discover if any epiphanies or other ideas build on what you previously wrote. If you are so inclined, instead of writing thoughts down, have a conversation with yourself while recording on tape or disk. Play back your recording – you may be surprised what further thoughts surface next! Following each review, end the time with your choice of prayer, meditation, or just pure quiet.

After you feel you have adequately recognized and addressed these questions, see if you can compose a declaration of beliefs, whether you are working on yourself or enabling a dying patient. Using all of the notes and/or recordings that you have created, search for the high points and try to assimilate what spiritual ideals were both reviewed and discovered by forming sentences that begin with "I believe." For example, one might say, "I believe that I was put here to learn," "I believe that I won't die alone," or "I believe that I am loved by a Higher Power." When the declaration of beliefs is completed, display it where it can be easily seen on a daily basis as a quiet reminder of what is valued and should be honored by how we conduct our lives from day to day.

But what if you or a dying person says that they have no beliefs? There is still the opportunity for exploration of the self, and in doing so, spirituality may yet emerge. It may not be a spiritual form that others typically follow, but it can nevertheless be authentic and can provide meaning, sustenance, and purpose to daily life. David Elkins, PhD, in his book, *Beyond Religion: A Personal Program For Building a Spiritual Life Outside the Walls of Traditional Religion,* suggests that one can discover spiritual experiences that nurture the soul in unexpected paths. These can be in activities such as movies, music, poems, vacations, intimate relationships, etc. He suggests that one begins by identifying an activity that has in the past met a need at the core of your being. Next, indulge in a relaxing, pleasant fantasy on that activity, noticing the essential ingredient that was so nurturing for you. Then ask yourself what that fantasy told you was needed to nourish your soul, and choose to perform related but specific activities in the coming days. It could be reading a beloved book again, singing a favorite song, telling a story you love, or just spending time with a special person in your life. For those in good health, it may be returning to a favorite vacation spot, going to a concert, walking in the woods, and so on. As these activities are performed, journaling can be done for private reflection and consideration of further alternative paths to personal spirituality (Elkins 1998, pp.265–73).

For the person who now has their declaration of beliefs formed, the next step is to perform a self-examination of the present moment. At this time in your life, are you at peace with yourself? Are you at peace with others, or do you feel a need to "clear the air" or ask forgiveness from a particular person you feel you have wronged? Do you feel a need for reconciliation with either a person, situation, or belief? What specific thing can you do to achieve this reconciliation? It may be gathering information for clarification of new ideals, speaking directly to a person you sense estrangement from, or expressing repentance to a Higher Power. But no matter what the personal issue is, the goal is to ensure that one is in alignment with the spiritual beliefs that have been declared and chosen to embrace as guidelines for living life. If a barrier is discovered within that hampers serenity, one must act on it. By eradicating past blocks that shadow our existence, we are free to live more abundantly the beliefs that ring true in our being and that help to define who we are and what we desire to be as individuals.

The final step in this spiritual process is to go back to the where this all began, to the particular NDA behavior that occurred. Is it now easier to understand and accept what happened, now that spiritual ideals have been refurbished? Can the NDA experience now be viewed differently, possibly as a beautiful gift from beyond? It is important for a spiritual helper to assist the dying in understanding and making conscious the personal NDA experience, if physical and mental circumstances allow, in how NDA fits within their spiritual beliefs. By finding value and meaning in what took place, one may find substantiation by comparing what is believed to what was actually experienced during NDA. There can emerge a lessening fear of death, and with it, a release of heaviness, resentment, and dread. Perspectives can dramatically shift to the realization that death is a passage, a necessary route to yet another chapter in being.

The essence of humankind is spiritual. Spiritual development is an innate evolutionary capacity of all of humanity, a movement toward wholeness, an integral part of our existence. Just as our physical bodies naturally grow and develop, the capacity for spiritual growth is as normal and intrinsic as biological human life (Grof and Grof 1990, pp.1, 34). No matter what the personal beliefs are, every human being exists with a spiritual center within his or her being that can function as a sacred compass. That compass can be either totally ignored, dusted off and utilized at sporadic times, referred to on a fairly regular basis, or even shined and adjusted to its optimum performance as a daily guide. The choice is yours in how you use it in your life. Have you at times forgotten that you possess that spiritual core? We rarely neglect the needs of our bodies and our emotions as we function through a typical day. If we can make a concerted effort to include this spiritual portion of our humanity into daily roles and tasks that arise, life can suddenly seem to have renewed purpose and significant intention. It can offer possibilities for greater fulfillment, a more satisfied sense of personal achievement, and a hope for continued peaceful existence within a universe full of possibilities.

Conclusion – What Can Be Learned From Nearing Death Awareness?

Nearing Death Awareness (NDA) is a concept presently recognized primarily by staff and caregivers in some nursing homes, hospitals, and hospices. I have written this book in the hope that not only medical personnel but also – especially – the general public will become familiar with the phenomenon. Knowledge of what NDA is, what typical NDA behaviors are and how to respond appropriately can assist people in providing valuable support and comfort, as well as foster preparedness for their own passing when the time comes. Caregivers and loved ones with an open-minded perspective are even more effectively equipped to nurture spiritual growth for the dying in their last days, an immeasurable service deserved by all who pass from this life to the next.

What can be gained from a transpersonal view of NDA? Throughout human history, death has been viewed primarily as an event of excruciating emotional and sometimes physical pain for the dying one. I believe that the characteristics of NDA can present death from a larger perspective, supporting the transpersonal tradition. The human life inevitably undergoes dramatic shifts with time, such as a new job, moving to a new place, a change in marital status, arrival of children, etc. These changes can be stressful moments that sometimes contain feelings of despair and fear, but are usually followed by acceptance and a continuation of life experiences. Death can also be perceived the same way in a larger context. It can be seen as a passage, a necessary and expected shift in existence, but not a hopeless end to all of life; a route that segues into continued existence in another dimension.

My transpersonal view of death looks at the big picture, encompassing what is beyond and not always readily apparent in this physical life, viewing our existence as a part of a Oneness of life. A Divine wholeness, or Higher Power, radiates across different levels of existence, and can be manifested in different levels of consciousness. NDA behaviors such as symbolic language, visions/visitations, and pre-death dreams seem to support this transpersonal stance.

Hospice nurses Anne Sharp and Susan Terbay offer the vision of death as "a profound process of personal and spiritual discovery in the journey of each individual soul toward enlightenment" (Sharp and Terbay 1997, p.2). As the journey is undertaken, we learn of our interconnectedness in a purposeful universe so large we cannot fathom it (Wills-Brandon 2000, p.278). Death takes on a smaller role within this broader perspective. A connection seems to continue between those of us on earth and those who are living in a domain other than the physical life we know, thus robbing death of its prevailing negativity.

Elizabeth Kübler-Ross, in her work, *Death: The Final Stage of Growth*, states that for those who seek to understand death, it can become a highly creative force, encouraging the highest spiritual values of life. Instead of being a destructive, horrendous event, death can be seen as one of the most constructive and creative fundamentals of life and culture. If one summons the courage to deal with it and accept its presence when it surfaces, growth will occur. By going through the experience with someone else, one can gain acceptance, become more at peace with death, and be able to face continued life more meaningfully (Kübler-Ross 1975, pp.1–2, 117–18). Loved ones and care providers who are receptive to alternative ways of thinking during the dying process have increased ability to move past the sense of loss that can otherwise thwart happiness and serenity. In addition, they can be helpful servants to the dying in functioning as sources of strength and enlightenment.

NDA has powerful implications that support the concept of an afterlife. When symbolic language occurs, the dying seem to be metaphorically sharing an inherent knowledge of an indescribable channel to another realm that is unseen on earth, and appear to be lovingly and irresistibly drawn to "the other side." Their statements may hint at a need for closure in relationships and situations. Dreams can also echo subconscious concerns, often repeating themes until they are acknowledged and addressed. Visitations from deceased loved ones, religious figures, and Divine Beings frequently appear in dreams, but also may appear in the sickroom. These gestures and motivations seem to be divinely supportive in nature, preparing and nurturing the dying for gentle movement to another dimension.

My mother stimulated my inquiry into the concept of NDA when she appeared to be actively dying. Up to that point, I had the common antipathy towards, and fear of death, and saw the prospect of my mother's passing to be totally overwhelming, hopeless, and unbearable. After witnessing her NDA behavior and educating myself about its possible causes, my perspective towards death has now been greatly modified, and my personal faith powerfully strengthened. Whether knowingly or unknowingly, my mother was a beacon of enlightenment, serving as a model for NDA behavior while teaching her daughter about what is beyond. During those moments when she spoke of unseen people and reached for unseen objects, I experienced first-hand the essence of a holy transcendence in the room, the presence of a loving Force quietly stroking our souls, offering both of us comfort and spiritual growth.

One of my mother's hospice workers once said, "She's got one foot on either side of the fence." I have often thought that her statement clearly described NDA: Nearing Death Awareness behavior is the fence, with this physical life on one side and an unknown, new dimension on the other. The dying, in straddling the fence, can look back at their lives in retrospect and preparation, yet see glimpses over the fence of the numinous place they are about to travel to. The dying are blessed by experiencing that unique point of reference, and witnesses to the dying have the priceless opportunity to use the duality of the dying experience as an impetus for spiritual review, discovery, and growth. Family, friends, and caregivers can receive an unexpected heavenly "appetizer," effectively stimulating their spiritual hunger for a broader perspective on existence and more importantly, a greater sense of Oneness with their Creator. Spiritual ideals can be refined with a renewed intent of a more fulfilling and productive existence on this earth.

References

a' Kempis, T. (1967) *The Imitation of Christ.* New York: Sheed and Ward. (Original work published 1473.)

Alcott, L.M. (1913) "Life, Letters, and Journals of Louisa May Alcott." From 1889, as excerpted in *Journal of the American Society for Psychical Research 7*, July 1913. (Original work published 1891.)

Anderson, C. (2002) "A.J., on dying." *Journal of Hospice and Palliative Nursing 3*, 180–3. Available at http://nursingcenter.com/library/JournalArticle.asp?Article_ID=285733.

Atwater, P.M.H. (1988) *Coming Back to Life: The After-Effects of the Near-Death Experience.* New York: Ballantine Books.

Atwater, P.M.H. (1995) *Beyond the Light: The Mysteries and Revelations of Near-Death Experiences.* New York: Avon Books.

Atwater, P.M.H. (2005) *We Live Forever: The Real Truth About Death.* Virginia Beach, Virginia: A.R.E. Press.

Barrett, W. (1926) *Death-Bed Visions: The Psychical Experiences of the Dying.* London: Psychic Press.

Bedard, G. and Callanan, M. (2003) *Final Gifts: An Interview With Maggie Callanan on Nearing Death Awareness.* Near-Death Newsletter. Accessed at www.near-death.com/newsletters/2003/02.html.

Beil, G.K. (1998) "Looking for Dr. Farmer." Paper presented to the Texas State Historical Association, March 1998 meeting. Available at www.cets.sfasu.edu/Harrison/Farmer/tsha.htm.

Bernard, J.S., and Schneider, M. (1996) *The True Work of Dying: A Practical and Compassionate Guide to Easing the Dying Process.* New York: Avon Books.

Boerstler, R.W. and Kornfeld, H.S. (1995) *Life to Death: Harmonizing the Transition.* Rochester, Vermont: Healing Arts Press.

Boss, M. (1958) *The Analysis of Dreams.* New York: Philosophical Library.

Browne, M.T. (1994) *Life After Death: A Renowned Psychic Reveals What Happens to Us When We Die.* New York: Ballantine Books.

Bulkeley, K. and Bulkley, P. (2005) *Dreaming Beyond Death: A Guide to Pre-Death Dreams and Visions.* Boston, Massachusetts: Beacon Press.

Byock, I. (1997) *Dying Well: Peace and Possibilities at the End of Life.* New York: Riverhead Books.

Callanan, M. and Kelley, P. (1997) *Final Gifts: Understanding the Special Awareness, Needs and Communications of the Dying.* New York: Bantam Books. (Original work published 1992.)

Coberly, M. (2002) *Sacred Passage: How to Provide Fearless, Compassionate Care for the Dying.* Boston, Massachusetts: Shambhala Publications.

Colarusso, C.A. (2005) "The Evolution of Paternal Identity in Late Adulthood." *Journal of the American Psychoanalytic Association 53,* 1, 51–81. Available at www.apsa.org/Portals/1/docs/JAPA/JAPAauthors.htm.

Crookall, R. (1964) *More Astral Projections: Analyses of Case Histories.* London: Aquarian Press.

Crystal, E. (2006) *Edgar Cayce.* Available at www.crystalinks.com/edgar_cayce.html, Part 4.

Denwiddie, V. (2003) "Review of the Book *Dreams Are Letters From the Soul.*" Intuitive Connections. Available at www.intuitive-connections.net/2003/book-dreamsoul.htm.

Elkins, D.N. (1998) *Beyond Religion: A Personal Program For Building A Spiritual Program Outside the Walls of Traditional Religion.* Wheaton, Illinois: Quest Books.

Endlink – Resource for End of Life Care Education (2006) *Spiritual Pain/Spiritual Suffering.* Chicago, Illinois: Endlink. Available at http://endlink.lurie.northwestern.edu/religion_spirituality/pain.cfm.

Flammarion, C. (1921) *Death and its Mystery: Before Death – Proofs of the Existence of the Soul.* Vol. 1. New York: The Century Co.

Flammarion, C. (1922) *Death and its Mystery: At the Moment of Death.* Vol. 2. New York: The Century Co.

Flammarion, C. (1923) *Death and its Mystery: After Death.* Vol. 3. New York: The Century Co.

Fourtier, M.K. (1972) *Dreams and Preparation for Death.* Ann Arbor, Michigan: University Microfilms.

Frejer, B.E. (1999) *The Edgar Cayce Companion: A Comprehensive Treatise of the Edgar Cayce Readings.* Virginia Beach, Virginia: A.R.E. Press. (Original work published 1996.)

Gallup Jr., G., with Proctor, W. (1982) *Adventures in Immortality: A Look Beyond the Threshold of Death.* New York: McGraw-Hill.

Grof, C. and Grof, S. (1990) *The Stormy Search for the Self: A Guide to Personal Growth Through Transformational Crisis.* New York: Tarcher/Penguin.

Guenther, M. (1995) *Toward Holy Ground: Spiritual Directions in the Second Half of Life.* Boston, Massachusetts: Cowley Publications.

Hascup, V.A. (2006) *Nearing Death Awareness.* King of Prussia, Pennsylvania: Merion Publications. Available at www.advanceweb.com.

Hayward, J. and Varela, F.J. (1992) *Gentle Bridges: Conversations with the Dalai Lama on the Sciences of the Mind.* Boston, Massachusetts: Shambhala Publications.

Holder, J.S. and Aldredge-Clanton, J. (2004) *Parting: A Handbook for Spiritual Care Near the End of Life.* Chapel Hill, North Carolina: University of North Carolina Press.

Hospice of the Florida Suncoast (2006) *Nearing Death Awareness.* Clearwater, Florida: The Hospice of the Florida Suncoast. Available at www.thehospice.org.deathaware.htm.

Hoholik, S. (2004) "Study Says Patient Can't Hold Off Death, But Stories Disagree." In *The Columbus Dispatch,* December 22.

Huxley, A. (1945) *The Perennial Philosophy.* New York: Harper and Row.

IANDS (2006a) *Impact of the Near-Death Experience on Grief and Loss.* East Windsor Hill, Connecticut: The International Association For Near-Death Studies, Inc. Available at www.iands.org/grief_and_loss.html.

IANDS (2006b) *What is a Near-Death Experience?* East Windsor Hill, Connecticut: The International Association for Near-Death Studies, Inc. Available at www.iands.org/nde_index.php.

IANDS (2006c) *Ascension.* East Windsor Hill, Connecticut: The International Association For Near-Death Studies, Inc. Available at www.iands.org/ascension.html.

IANDS (2006d) *Life/Death?.* East Windsor Hill, Connecticut: The International Association For Near-Death Studies, Inc. Available at www.iands.org/berk.html.

Jacobi, J.S. (1962) *The Psychology of C.G. Jung: An Introduction with Illustrations.* Translated by R. Manheim. New Haven, Connecticut: Yale University Press.

Jung, C.G. (1975) *Memories, Dreams, Reflections.* New York: Pantheon Books. (Original work published 1963.)

Kearney, M. (1996) *Mortally Wounded: Stories of Soul Pain, Death, and Healing.* New York: Scribner.

Kessler, D. (2000) *The Needs of the Dying: A Guide for Bringing Hope, Comfort, and Love to Life's Final Chapter.* New York: HarperCollins.

Khan, M.Z. (trans.) (1997) *The Qur'an.* New York: Olive Branch Press. (Original work published 1975.)

Kircher, P.M. and Callanan, M. (2003) *Nearing Death Awareness in the Terminally Ill.* East Windsor Hill, Connecticut: The International Association For Near-Death Studies, Inc. Available at www.iands.org/terminally_ill.html.

Kraybill, B.M. (2005) *Nearing Death Awareness.* PERT Program Tip of the Month, January 2005. Swedish Medical Center. Available at www.swedishmedical.org/PERT/tip/.htm.

Kübler-Ross, E. (1975) *Death: The Final Stage of Growth.* New York: Simon and Schuster, Inc.

Kübler-Ross, E. (1991) *On Life After Death.* Berkeley, California: Celestial Arts.

Kübler-Ross, E. (1997a) *On Death and Dying: What the Dying Have to Teach Doctors, Nurses, Clergy, and Their Own Families.* New York: Touchstone Books. (Original work published 1970.)

Kübler-Ross, E. (1997b) *Questions and Answers on Death and Dying.* New York: Touchstone. (Original work published 1974.)

Kuhl, D. (2002) *What Dying People Want: Practical Wisdom for the End of Life.* Cambridge, Massachusetts: Perseus Books.

Long, J.A and Long, J.P. (2006) *Spiritual Spectrum Stories: Spiritually Transforming Events, Prayer, Nearing End of Life Events.* Out of Body Research Foundation. Available at www.oberf.org/ste_prayer_nele.htm.

Martin, J. and Romanowski, P. (1997) *Love Beyond Life: The Healing Power of After-Death Communications.* New York: HarperCollins.

Matt, D.C. (trans.) (1983) *Zohar, the Book of Enlightenment.* New York: Paulist Press.

Miller, J.E., with Cutshall, S.C. (2001) *The Art of Being a Healing Presence.* Fort Wayne: Willowgreen Publishing.

Moody, R. (2001) *Life After Life: The Investigation of a Phenomenon – Life After Death.* San Francisco, California: Harper Books. (Original work published 1975.)

Morse, M. with Perry, P. (1990) *Closer to the Light: Learning from the Near-Death Experiences of Children.* New York: Random House.

Morse, M. with Perry, P. (1994) *Parting Visions: Uses and Meanings of Pre-Death, Psychic, and Spiritual Experiences.* New York: Villard Books.

Moss, R. (2003) *Active Dreaming to Help the Dying.* Portland, Oregon: New Connexion – Journal of Conscious Living. Available at www.newconnexion.net/article/index/cfm.

Osis, K. and Haraldsson, E. (1977) *At the Hour of Death.* New York: Avon Books.

Peele, S. (2002) *An Angelic Visit.* Venture Inward, November 22 2002. Virginia Beach, Virginia: The Association for Research and Enlightenment. Available at www.edgarcayce.org/venture_inward/11122002/article.

Powers, J. (1995) "Death and Dying in Tibetan Buddhism." In *Introduction to Tibetan Buddhism.* Ithaca, New York: Snow Lion Publications.

Prabhupada, A.C.B. (1986) *Bhagavad-Gita As It Is.* Los Angeles, California: The Bhaktivedanta Book Trust. (Original work published 1972.)

Raines, H. (1983) *My Soul is Rested: The Story of the Civil Rights Movement in the Deep South.* New York: Penguin Books. (Original work published 1977.)

Reed, H. (2006) *Do Dreams Have Meaning?* Available at www.creativespirit.net/ henryreed/meaning.htm

Reitman, V. (2004) "Taking Life's Final Exit." In *Los Angeles Times,* June 14.

Remen, R.N. (1997) *Kitchen Table Wisdom.* New York: Riverhead Books.

Remen, R.N. and Toms, M. (2001) *Mystery: The Wisdom of the Soul.* Carlsbad, California: Hay House. Audio-cassette.

Rhodes, L. (1997) *Tunnel to Eternity: Beyond Near-Death.* West Chester, Pennsylvania: Chrysalis Books.

Rusnak, K.J. (2006) *The World of the Dying.* Available at www.thebrickwall2.com/twotd.htm.

Sharp, A.W. and Terbay, S.H. (1997) *Gifts: Two Hospice Professionals Reveal Messages From Those Passing On.* Far Hills, New Jersey: New Horizon Press.

Singh, K.D. (2000) *The Grace in Dying.* San Francisco, California: HarperCollins. (Original work published 1998.)

Storm, H. (2005) *My Descent Into Death: A Second Chance at Life.* New York: Doubleday Books.

Underwood, A. (2005) "Review of the Book *A Dream Before Dying.*" Newsweek, July 25 2005. Available at www.msnbc.msn.com/id/8598959/site/newsweek.

UPI (2006) *Near-Death Survivors Recall the Other Side.* United Press International Religion and Spirituality Forum, June 30. Available at http://religionandspirituality.com- currentEvents/view.php?StoryID= 20060630–072535–3706r

Van de Castle, R.L. (1994) *Our Dreaming Mind.* New York: Ballantine Books.

Van der Post, L. (1975) *Jung and the Story of Our Time.* New York: Pantheon Books.

Von Franz, M.L. (1987) *On Dreams and Death: A Jungian Interpretation.* Boston, Massachusetts: Shambhala Books.

Watkins, M. (1984) *Waking Dreams.* Dallas, Texas: Spring Publications, Inc. (Original work published 1976.)

Weber, R. (ed.) (1990) *Dialogues with Scientists and Sages: The Search for Unity.* New York: Arcana Books. (Original work published 1986.)

Wilber, K. (1985) *No Boundary: Eastern and Western Approaches to Personal Growth.* Boston, Massachusetts: Shambhala Publications. (Original work published 1979.)

Wilber, K. (1996) *Up From Eden: A Transpersonal View of Human Evolution.* Wheaton, Illinois: Quest Books. (Original work published 1981.)

Wills-Brandon, C. (2000) *One Last Hug Before I Go: The Mystery and Meaning of Deathbed Visions.* Deerfield Beach, Florida: Health Communications, Inc.

Wills-Brandon, C. (2006) *Death Bed Visions.* Ontario: ParaResearchers of Ontario. Available at www.pararesearchers.org/Psychic/dbv/dbv.html.

Wooten-Green, R. (2005) *The Symbolic Language of the Dying: Metaphor and Meaning.* Sacramento, California: California Catholic Conference. Available at www.embracingourdying.com/articles/symbolic.html.

Wooten-Green, R. and Champlin, J.M. (2001) *When the Dying Speak: How to Listen To and Learn From Those Who Face Death.* Chicago, Illinois: Loyola Press.

Young, D.C. and Hade, E.M. (2004) "Holidays, Birthdays, and Postponement of Cancer Death." *Journal of the American Medical Association 292,* 24, 3012–3016.

Subject Index

Author Index